Wild River Guide
to Coastal Waterways

from Corolla to Cape Henry

Also by Lillie Gilbert and Vickie Shufer

Wild River Guide to North Landing River
and its tributaries
ISBN: 0-938423-06-1
978-0-938426-06-5

Wild River Guide to Dismal Swamp Water Trails
including waterways of northeastern North Carolina
ISBN: 0-938423-11-8
978-0-938426-11-9

Here's what reviewers had to say about the
Wild River Guide to Coastal Waterways from Corolla to Cape Henry

A thorough guide to paddling the Atlantic Flyway from Currituck Sound to Cape Henry. Shufer and Gilbert invite the urban dweller to live and breathe nature and local history at their finest. I can't think of a better way to spend a weekend!

Edna Baden, Executive Director
The Whalehead Club Currituck Heritage Park

A lovely guide for the local paddler and full of information for the outsider, its history makes it an enjoyable read even before you put in the water.

Sharon A. Meade, Curator/Visitor Services
Outer Banks Center for Wildlife Education

In the 16 years that I have lived and worked in Virginia Beach, I am constantly amazed at the diversity of our history and of the paddling opportunities that exist here. Once again, I find myself transported on a series of journeys taken by Lillie and Vickie that serve as guides to the opportunities for adventure and history that are in our very own backyard. The new book is a page turner for paddlers and history buffs alike.

Ron Kuhlman, V.P. Tourism Marketing & Sales
Virginia Beach Convention & Visitors Bureau

Vickie and Lillie are the perfect people to write this book. This paddler's guide is so much more: from launch and landing sites androutes along the way we see the history of the area along with the points of interest from a naturalist's point of view. Even the armchair adventurer will find this book enlightening.

Fielding Lewis Tyler, Executive Director
Old Coast Guard Station, Virginia Beach, VA

What a tremendous new book for paddlers wishing to partake of the beauty, history and environmental diversity of our regional waterways. Once again, Lillie and Vickie have provided a delightful guide on the wonders of our watershed from Cape Henry to Corolla. This is a must read for all who cherish and enjoy our natural environment.

Cindy Curtis, CPRP Director
City of Virginia Beach, Department of Parks and Recreation

Wild River Guide to Coastal Waterways

from Corolla to Cape Henry

Number 3 in a Series of Guidebooks for Paddlers, Naturalists and Historians

by Lillie Gilbert and Vickie Shufer

Virginia Beach, Virginia

Published by:
ECO IMAGES
P.O. Box 61413
Virginia Beach, VA 23466-1413
757.421.3929
Email: EcoImages@cox.net
www.ecoimages-us.com

ISBN 978-0-938423-17-1

Copies of this book are available from
WILD RIVER OUTFITTERS, INC.
3636 Virginia Beach Blvd. #108
Virginia Beach, VA 23452
Phone: 757.431.8566
Toll Free: 877.431.8566
Fax: 757.340.1098
Email: mail@wildriveroutfitters.com
URL: www.wildriveroutfitters.com

Printed in the United States of America

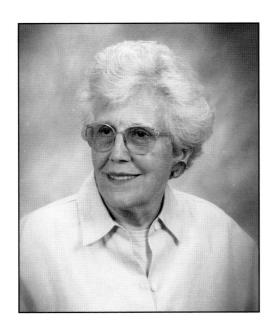

Dedicated to Elizabeth Baum Hanbury,
historian, writer, educator, gracious lady
and generous friend to all who knew her.
Elizabeth had deep roots in the
coastal water, land and its people.

Table of Contents

Waterway Map Contents

Acknowledgments

Very special thanks go to Anne Henry, long-time friend, who spent hours proofreading, found resource material, recalled memories of Virginia Beach, and generously shared information we could not have found elsewhere. Julie Pouliot and Fielding Tyler of the Old Coast Guard Station also spent hours relating information and shared photographs and resource information. Their enthusiasm to lend help was immeasurable. Melinda and Reese Lukei loaned original writings and proofread some of the sections of the book. Reese related waterway information during a canoeing trip on Back Bay. Deni Norred would always proofread when we got in a jam and needed just the right word. The Martin family cannot be thanked enough for their generous use of their waterfront orchards and vineyards for many paddling trips from Knotts Island.

The Virginia Beach Department of Parks and Recreation was never hesitant to share information and photographs about the access points and park areas related to these waterways. Pat Ricks, former owner of Blue Pete's Restaurant, allowed the generous use of his property for ecotours and personal kayaking trips for over fifteen years. We also thank KC Knauer and her family, who are current owners of Blue Pete's for allowing us to continue to use their property for tours and dining afterward. Thanks go to Eve Estes Butts, Susan Admire and the members of the Back Bay Restoration Foundation for educating our city's citizens and for helping to conserve an important ecosystem and watershed.

Belinda Nash loaned books by Louisa Venable Kyle and offered a lot of insight and information about Grace Sherwood. Travis Morris shared memories of duck hunting and daughter, Rhonda Morris, was a willing kayaker guide and shared memories of going into the Monkey Island Club as a child. Rhonda loaned many history books about coastal Carolina and in particular *Currituck Legacy*, a book about her family genealogy, the Baum family, written by Elizabeth Hanbury. It is because of this Baum family book and calling Elizabeth for information that the authors came to know Mrs. Hanbury. Elizabeth shared many memories and much information on a driving tour of part of Currituck County and the Outer and Inner Banks of North Carolina when we were doing research for this book. Edna Baden, Executive Director of the Whalehead Club, proofread the information about the Whalehead Club, gave us private tours of the Whalehead Club and went kayaking with us in Currituck Sound. Edna and Jill Landen, Curator of The Whalehead Club were generous in loaning photos for this book. Paddlers on our many cruises and "recon" missions were Geney Ross, Gary Knapp, Stephanie Herron, Judy Roehling, Reese Lukei, Rhonda Morris, Sandy Baylor, Ginger Power, Dru Ferrence and members of the OBX paddling club, Linda Knowles, Deni Norred, Nancy Andrews, Lorainne Eaton and others whose names we may have forgotten or failed to mention. Thanks also to proofreader, Laura Anderson who gave us several very helpful suggestions. Thanks to Peregrine Outfitters who gave us the trusty purple canoe from which we conducted all of our quiet water paddle research. Heartfelt thanks to Gilbert Keene for a wonderful boat ride on the Eastern Branch of the Lynnhaven and Penny Brown for enthusiasm and encouragement.

Thanks to Joe Thornton for acting as a guide and informant for Carova, the community south of False Cape State Park, to Richard MacFetters, volunteer at Mackay Island National Wildlife Refuge, for giving us a personal tour of the refuge and providing us with some local history. Thanks to Kyle Barbour and Cameron Swain at False Cape State Park for sharing their vast knowledge of the area and to the staff at Back Bay National Wildlife Refuge as well. Above all, I (Vickie) have to thank Paul, my husband, who has spent many late hours after coming home from work to convert the many images in this book to color-separated duotones. Without his help, the book just wouldn't be the same.

Special thanks to all of the folks who contribute to the various foundations, clubs, history societies, and governmental and non-profit organizations who do so much for our environment and our historic places. You know who you are and you are doing the right thing! Keep up the excellent work! After all, it is for you that we have written this book and hope you find it helpful and informative as you explore our coastal waterways.

Preface

Rich in history and loved by locals, these waterways are indeed special. We have paddled some of these little creeks for many years and have never had a thought that we would not have a great day. Somehow these waterways always supply us with a refreshing new view. Whether it's a different season or a different time of day, the sunlight sparkles differently on the water, a plant presents itself in bloom, a new bird calls, a deer or raccoon scampers away and the quiet is momentarily interrupted.

If you are new to paddling or thinking about getting into it, do. If you are already a paddler, enjoy getting to know these creeks and bays in new ways. We are offering a look at our backyard that we hope will provide the reader, paddler or not, with some interesting tidbits of natural and historical information. Hopefully, through education, comes understanding; with understanding, appreciation; and with appreciation, preservation. Help us save what we still have left to treasure.

While we try very hard to get our facts straight, please let us know if there should be changes. We welcome your input.

Note from Lillie: On a sunny fall morning in 1969, a friend called to ask if I'd like to join in on a jeep ride down the beach. Without hesitation or any knowledge of where we were headed, I said, "Sure!" Four of us and a dog roared off Sandbridge beach and headed to North Carolina. I remember a highlight was finding our way along the sand through the old stumps, reminders of a long buried forest. The beach was rutted with other tire tracks and the ride was incredibly bumpy. We probably drove way too fast, but we were so young and carefree. The second memorable site was the old Currituck Lighthouse which we found through a tangle of trees and shrubs on an old dirt road. The area was so overgrown I do not even remember seeing the Whalehead Club at all. The keeper's house was in bad need of repair and paint. We were disappointed that we could not climb the lighthouse as the entrance was boarded up. Thirty-five years later, I finally climbed the lighthouse and looked at the magnificent view that I wished about so long ago. I would imagine that the former look without so much development was much more interesting, but the magical draw of coastal waterways has fascinated me ever since.

Note from Vickie: It was spring, 1979 that I arrived in Virginia Beach to work as a naturalist interpreter at Seashore State Park, now First Landing State Park, an area rich in natural and cultural history. I was intrigued with the area and immersed myself in learning as much as I could. Exploring the coastal waterways was a part of my educational experience and I approached it with gusto. My first experience at False Cape State Park was on the back of a park pick-up truck going over mountains of sand dunes, which at that time was one of the east-west roads from the beach into the park. It was love at first sight. Since then I have led many groups, both by kayak and on foot into both First Landing and False Cape State Parks to share what I have learned about the area. While First Landing State Park is located in the northernmost part of the city, False Cape is in the southernmost part of the city. Exploring the waterways that lie between these two parks and continuting south into Currituck County has provided a more complete picture of the area and the people who live here.

Every paddling trip is a new adventure and we hope that this book will help guide you into experiencing your own adventures and that you will enjoy it as much as we enjoyed the research on and off the water to produce it for you.

Introduction

In our book, Wild River Guide to Dismal Swamp Water Trails, we describe paddling sections on the western side of the Currituck Sound, going as far south as Poplar Branch Landing. In this book, we are beginning with Poplar Branch Landing as an access/destination point and continuing north into Currituck County on the eastern side of Currituck Sound in North Carolina and proceeding north toward Knotts Island Bay and Back Bay in Virginia. The entire scope of this book will be inland coastal paddling as well as along the oceanfront in Virginia Beach, Virginia to Cape Henry which is the entrance to the Chesapeake Bay, and around the cape into the Lynnhaven.

Any inside paddling of the Inner Banks would not be complete without descriptions of several of the numerous islands which provide interesting exploring and observations. We have chosen those with interesting history, extraordinary flora or fauna, or simply those which make promising stop-overs for a day of boating enjoyment.

While we have researched and paddled this area for years, we realize that there are always omissions or corrections that could be changed. We invite your comments and encourage you to visit this area which still has much wildness.

Part 1

Currituck Sound

Currituck Sound

Even though the Currituck Sound is a large body of water, ranging from 1000 feet to 6000 feet across in some areas, the depth is fairly shallow, being only three or four feet in many places. This can present problems when the wind picks up, resulting in choppy waters and even waves breaking at times. Do check the weather forecast before venturing out.

Numerous islands, ponds, coves and creeks lie just off the western shoreline of the Currituck Banks, north of the Currituck/Dare County line. Interesting names have been given to these areas and are still known to the local fishermen today who use them to designate fishing areas. Even though the islands are private, paddling around them can be fun with a lot of opportunities for observing wildlife.

Location

Currituck Sound is located in Currituck County, beginning north of Kitty Hawk in North Carolina. It stretches north to Knotts Island Bay and Back Bay and to North Landing River to the northwest. To the south is the Albemarle Sound. It is bordered on the east by the Currituck Banks and on the west by the Currituck County mainland.

Access Points

A. **Poplar Branch Landing**
B. **Whalehead Club in Corolla**

Paddling under the walkway bridge at the Whalehead Club into Whale Head Bay

vs

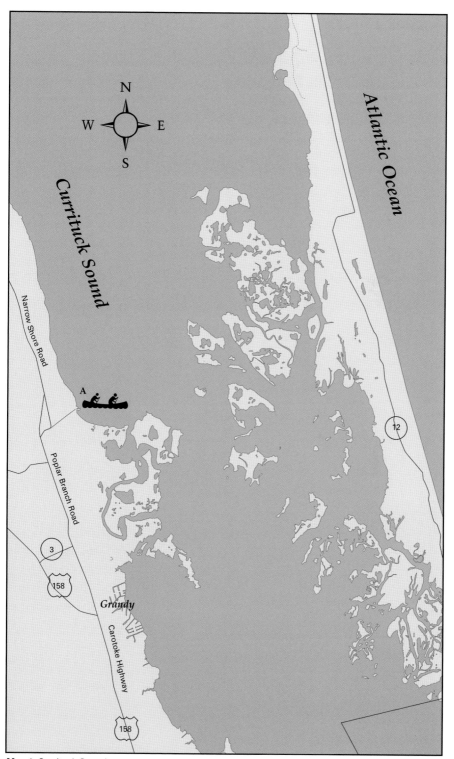

Map 1: Currituck Sound

3

© Vickie Shufer

Access Points
A. *Poplar Branch Landing*

Directions: From U.S. Route 158/Carotoke Highway, just north of Grandy, turn east on Route 1131/Poplar Branch Road. If driving from the north, turn east on SR 3 and then north on Route 1131/Poplar Branch Road. The road will dead end at the public boat landing.

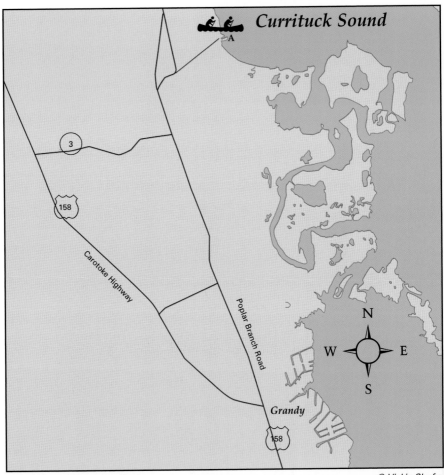

Map 2: Poplar Branch Landing   © Vickie Shufer

The river is the center of the land, the place where the waters, and much more, come together. Here is the home of wildlife, the route of explorers, and recreation paradise...Only fragments of our inheritance remain unexploited, but these streams are more valuable than ever.

Tim Palmer, *Lifelines*

B. Whalehead Club in Corolla

Directions: From NC 12 in Corolla, go north 2 miles and turn west (left) at Currituck Heritage Park. Continue west to the public boat ramp at the end of the road. The public launch site is a paved ramp just to the west of the Whalehead Club. Paddle trips from this location afford the canoeist or kayaker unlimited opportunities for exploring the waterways of Currituck Sound and nearby islands. An interesting photo opportunity is the rustic arched bridge leading the paddler into the boat house area pond with either the Whalehead Club or the Currituck Beach Lighthouse in the background.

Caution: Winds can come up quickly at any time of year and summer storms are common. Please do not overestimate one's ability when venturing across Currituck Sound. We highly recommend shorter trips around nearby islands or along the shoreline unless one is an experienced paddler and fully prepared. We also recommend a GPS or compass and marine chart. Do not forget to file a float plan with someone, notifying them of your intended destination and your expected return time.

Launch site at Whalehead Club

5

vs

Corolla – It's a Place, Not a Car

Corolla, North Carolina has a fascinating history. Before the village got its official name, it is reported that the old-timers that lived south of here called the Corolla neighborhood Whaleshead, supposedly for a giant of a whale that washed ashore. As the story goes, the whale's head was so large that a local man drove his horse and cart into the propped open mouth. The Corolla natives dropped the "s" and the place became known informally as Whalehead. It wasn't until the post office was official in the village that the place got a name that stuck. Suzanne Tate quotes Norris Austin in her book, *Whalehead, Tales of Corolla, N.C.*, as he relates the true story.

> ...Back in 1896 when the first post office was established here, and Emma Jones was the Postmaster, three names were sent in – Jones Beach, Whalehead and Currituck Beach. The Post Office Department didn't like the first two names, and there was already a Currituck Post Office. Then a teacher who lived here said, `The inner circle or petals of a flower are called the corolla.' Many violets grew wild here so people liked the name. It was sent in to the Post Office Department and accepted.
>
> The tourists I see everyday call our village CUH-ROLL-UH rather than CUH-RAWL-UH – the correct pronunciation. I like to say to them: the car industry has CUH-ROLL-UH- we in Corolla have the inner circle of a flower! (Tate, 1987)

Corolla got its start not as a fishing village, but through its tie with the U.S. Government. The Lighthouse Service brought several families to this most northern of the Carolina lighthouses. Three keeper's families were there at all times. See page--- for an early account of living beneath the beam of the Corolla Light.

Whaling History

The name of Currituck County's Whalehead Club Lodge may come from an  old local story concerning a whale that

© James Melvin

washed up on the nearby beach. Supposedly the whale was so huge that a fully rigged horse and buggy could fit inside its mouth. Whether this is a true tale about the whale's size or not, there have been many whales that have washed up on the Atlantic shore in Carolina and Virginia. There was a life-saving station located ⅞ of a mile north of the Currituck Light first called Life-Saving Station No. 8, then the Jones Hill Station, and by 1894 it was called Whales Head Station. It was from a telegraph wire set up near the Whales Head Station that the news "Experiment successful Home Christmas" was relayed to the world on December 17, 1903 on behalf of the Wright brothers at Kitty Hawk (Hanbury, 1985).

Colonial records indicate that barrels of whale oil were shipped from coastal Carolina but it is unknown as to whether there was an organized industry yet or just the serendipitous work resulting from the beaching of whales. In 1670 Peter Carteret writes, "Very few whales came on Shoare wee made about 38 bar's [barrels] of Oile" (Powell, 1958). An account from Peter Carteret in 1672/3 states "At severall tymes I have Shipped one hundred nynty five Barrells of Whale Oyle for London and Consigned it to Sir Peter Colliton...I Conceive may have cleared about 25.s P barrell" (Powell, 1958). In 1681 an English court document changed an earlier decree of 1668 which had said that all results of whale fishing would "wholly belong to the Lords Proprietors." The 1681 proclamation said that "for the incouragement of Carolina" the inhabitants were authorized to take "what whales they can and convert them to their own use" (Powell, 1958). A court record of 1696 contains a petition of Charles Thomas who was "working on a Whale in March last; ten dayes and at last Mathias Towler tooke the said whale" and never paid Mr. Thomas for his work. The petitioner requested payment from Mr. Towler "for his labor after the rate of two Shillings p day" (Hathaway, 1900). Another recorded instance of whales coming ashore is from the Edinburgh newspaper, *Caledonian Mercury*, dated February 23, 1765. "They write from Cape Fear, in North Carolina, that seven whales, of the grampus kind, had, in December last, been cast on shore thro' the violence of Easterly winds; one of which measured 137 feet in length" (NC Archaeology Website, 2001).

In 1725, Samuel Chadwick was issued the first documented license to hunt whales. His license granted him the right to use "three boats to fish for Whale or Other Royall fish on ye Seay Coast of this government and whatsoever you catch to convert to your own use paying ye Hon. ye Governor one tenth parte of ye Oyls and bone Made by vertue of this License" (Barfield, 1995). The Chadwick family was from New England and eventually moved to North Carolina, settling in Carteret County, NC and descendants of this family live there today.

The native Bankers did not seek the whales from whaling boats as much as they simply waited, as John Brickell in the 1700s wrote in his *Natural History of North Carolina*, "upon Providence to throw those dead Monsters on Shoar, which frequently happens to great advantage and profit" (Barfield, 1995). Things changed sometime in the 19th century and near Cape Lookout, men camped out and waited for whale migrations in late winter and early spring. Boats would be launched through the surf with the hopes of bringing in a whale. These authors have not been able to locate documentation that shows organized whaling hunts off the Currituck Banks. We can only assume that the Bankers here relied on beached or stranded whales.

On Saturday, November 1, 1884, Julian Baum, the 14 year old son of Josephus Baum of Currituck County notes in his diary that, "Pa Jim and I went down to The Ocean and cut up a whale which came ashore Thursday. After dinner Pa and Grandpa made oil of the whale" (Hanbury, 1985). It seems quite plausible that the coast of North Carolina had stranded whales as it had stranded sailing ships, although from different causes. While sightseeing boats seeking whales are not popular along North Carolina's northernmost shores, just over the state line in nearby Virginia Beach, Virginia, whale watching has become a popular tourist attraction. See page 114 for more information.

Phantoms of the Sea

The waters off the Outer Banks are known as a ship graveyard and have been referred to as the "Graveyard of the Atlantic." Many books have been written about the wayward spirits who haunt the barrier islands. These are stories about ghosts of sailors drowned at sea, beach-goers who have died before their time, ghost dogs, and fishermen lost on the sound. The ghost ships, however, are particularly compelling. Two local reportings are listed below.

Two young men of Corolla were out late one night, hoping to catch a few unwitting fish. They settled in at their secret spot, very near the location of what was formerly called the "New" Currituck Inlet. The shifting sands of the Outer Banks had closed the inlet in 1828. The fishing was a bit slow, but the men remained silent so as to enhance their chances of coming home with breakfast fish. The wind had died and except for a few crickets and tree frogs, there was no other sound. Although there was no moon, they could see that the surface of the water was calm, clearly reflecting the trees along the shoreline where they sat, poles in hand. All of a sudden they caught a glimpse of something slowly coming closer. As if drifting in from the Atlantic Ocean, a fully rigged sailing vessel sailed past. The two young men were astonished. This made no sense. There was no wind. How could it sail? There was no inlet. How could it be moving from the direction it came? Needless to say, the two men fled quickly, the ghostly apparition firmly etched in their memories.

Another recounting of a phantom ship, the *Carol A Deering*, is found in many of the ghost tales of the Outer Banks. In the early 1920s, the five-masted schooner set sail from Bath, Maine on her maiden voyage. This ship and her crew never made port. Instead of being found in wreckage along this "Graveyard of the Atlantic," the *Deering* was unharmed. When the ship was located, it had run aground on Diamond Shoals. Searchers came by rowboats and called to the crew, but no one answered. Deciding to board the ship, they discovered that it was empty of all crew members. Not a soul was on board, alive or dead, except one fine cat. The *Deering* became known as the "ghost ship of Diamond Shoals." As to the disappearance of all hands on board, the mystery has never been solved.

U.S. Coast Guard Beach Patrol

By the fall of 1942, the footprints of the men of the Coast Guard who walked the beaches of coastal North Carolina and Virginia were joined by other prints in the sand: those of horses and dogs. Man's best friends were needed to supplement the watch. Intended acts of terrorism for the summer and fall of 1942 spurred the U.S. Government to action as it realized that the coastlines of the U.S. were largely unguarded. The untamed and sparsely populated Outer Banks provided many spots where intruders could be set ashore undetected.

Just as the Carolina and Virginia coasts offered seclusion for pirates of an earlier era, it was determined that the Nazi U-boats could unload rafts of men to infiltrate our country. Indeed, such was the case around midnight on June 14, 1942 when an inflatable raft with four men aboard was launched from a German submarine off Long Island, New York. Four days later, this time in Ponte Vedra, Florida, four men landed from a raft off a Nazi submarine. The eight different plans of terrorism that the eight men were to set in motion did not occur. Fortunately, for the citizens of the East Coast, all of the saboteurs were captured, but the outcome could have been horrifyingly different (Bishop, 1989).

The job of the U.S. Coast Guard Beach Patrol began in earnest as a directive of July 25, 1942 states, "These beach patrols are not intended as a military protection of our coastline, as this is a function of the Army. The beach patrols are more in the nature of outposts to report activities along the coastline and are not to repel hostile armed units." A great number of people living along the beaches and waterways were given the opportunity to assist and the government hired those able to train and work with horses and dogs. A wide variety of talent was amassed from age 17 to 73. Many people with German shepherd dogs donated them for enrollment in the Coast Guard Reserve although eighteen breeds were used by the joint training of Coast Guard and Army dogs. At the end of autumn, 1942, 2,000 dogs were in training and within a year 1,800 were patrolling not only beaches but Navy installations around the U.S.

Horses were next on the training schedule, coming months after the initial dog camps. The first horse patrols on the Atlantic and Gulf Coasts began in November of 1942 and December on the Pacific Coast. The Whalehead Club at Corolla, North Carolina was used as barracks as were several out buildings on the property. The Whalehead Club was built on elevated land and had a basement. It was here that the servicemen and their families were treated to movies. These could not be shown outside due to the light they created at night, which might show a U-boat where the coastline was and there was no movie theater at Corolla.

After 1944 when the Beach Patrol was disbanded, 23 dogs, 7 officers, and 21 enlisted men went to China to train the Chinese Army in the use of dogs and horses for patrol work. A full reporting of the work of the Beach Patrol is to be found in *Prints in the Sand: The U.S. Coast Guard Beach Patrol During World War II*, by Eleanor C. Bishop.

Currituck Heritage Park

The Currituck Heritage Park is located just off Highway 12 in Corolla. Winding walkways lead visitors to the Whalehead Club's original boathouse and pedestrian footbridge. The Currituck Beach Lighthouse and Light Keeper's House are located north of the boathouse. The Corolla Chapel (1885), Corolla Schoolhouse (1890) and Outer Banks Center for Wildlife Education (2005) are all within the park.

Whalehead Club

This large, stately home located near the Currituck Beach Lighthouse (also called Corolla Light) is on the west side of NC SR 12 in Corolla, NC. Built during 1922-1925, this elegant structure is now owned by Currituck County and has been restored by the Whalehead Preservation Trust for public tours. Originally built by Edward and Marie Louise Knight of Philadelphia as a private residence the property also contains a bridge and boathouse. The property now known as Currituck Heritage Park is located on property that originally housed the Lighthouse Club of Currituck Sound, organized in 1874 by a group of New York sportsmen who purchased the land from the local owners: Abraham Baum, Samuel Salyear, and Samuel McHorney. The adjacent Currituck Beach Lighthouse was begun in 1873 and completed in 1875. The small community around the lighthouse was first known as Jones Hill, then Currituck Beach. After 1895 when the first post office was opened, the area became known as Corolla (Hanbury, 1985). The club property sold in 1919 to L. W. Davis, W.A. Davis, and C.L. Davis who sold it in 1922 to Edward Collings Knight, Jr. who enjoyed duck hunting.

The Knights dredged a boat basin and two canals with the spoils used to build up the land upon which the house was to be built. Two arched bridges were constructed as access to the homesite. It was upon this higher ground that the Knights built a 36-room, 21,000 square foot palatial mansion complete with Tiffany lamps, an elevator, a library and four large fireplaces and five chimneys. The center chimney is false and was constructed to provide symmetry and ventilation throughout the house. The Knights* named their estate Corolla Island.

During construction, in April of 1923, an unusual object was unearthed. Mr. Knight wrote to F.D. Langenheim who was a contributor to the Academy of Natural Sciences of Philadelphia of the find.

Whalehead Club under construction

Photo Courtesy of Troy and Bill Lane

While dredging in the mud this afternoon, the scoop pulled up a large piece of something that looked like stone It was a shapeless mass (about seven feet in length) the only [thing] that was well defined was a hole that ran through it; a hole probably four inches in diameter. A few minutes later another piece was scooped up. The second piece was almost [identical] with the first, and having in it the same kind of hole or cavity. Both pieces were covered with barnacles and seashells, and proved to be bone, not stone. When placed side by side, while as I have already said, they were practically shapeless, they seemed to form the head of something. Of course everybody said it was the head of a whale and that it must, according to the size of the head bones, been a whale a hundred feet long. I have no idea what it is the head of. If it is that of a whale, then it must have been buried where we found it for many centuries; for the ocean in the last century, has been working in, not out. All along the beach to low tide one sees sticking out of the sand the stumps of trees, showing that in the days gone by what is now a beach was once a forest." (Davis, 2004)

The exterior of the house was built of cypress siding and cypress wood trim over eighteen-inch thick walls. The floors on the ground level were made of cork squares and the entry way walls were overlaid with small vertical strips of wood, both with the intent of keeping noise levels down and to present a "soft" look and feel. The doors were solid mahogany. The exterior was painted a bright yellow color to resemble a French country house. Mrs. Marie Louise LeBel Knight was French-Canadian and much of the interior design reflects her love of European fashion. The most striking external visual of this complex is the beautiful gambled roof of copper made as close to the original design as possible. The original copper roof was made of cut and molded copper strips made to resemble shingles (Bisher and Southern, 1996).

After the death of Mr. and Mrs. Knight in 1936, their heirs decided to put the entire property up for sale. Mr. Ray T. Adams purchased the property in 1940 for $25,000. It had cost the Knights $383,000 during the building period of 1922-25. It is Mr. Adams who renamed the property Whalehead Club. Travis Morris of Currituck remembers visiting the grand home in 1938 when his father was to accompany Mr. Adams on a tour of the house and grounds. "I remember going in that clubhouse the first time. All the furniture was covered with white sheets, but was uncovered for Mr. Adams inspection. I remember there was a grand piano, a safe with ducks and other wildlife on it that had come from the old Lighthouse Club, and I believe two grandfather clocks. The dining room had a long table and a long buffet" (Morris, 2006).

During World War II, the property was leased by Mr. Adams to the U.S. Coast Guard. After the war, the house became a retreat for Adams' guests to enjoy hunting, boating and the beach. Mr. Adams entertained many important political and military figures as well as a group of local boys.

The members of Boy Scout Troop 172, sponsored by Pilmoor United Methodist Church of Currituck, will never forget Mr. Adams or Corolla. For two summers, he gave us a week at the beach and let us stay in the Currituck Beach Coast Guard Station, which he then owned. The food we were served and the good times on the beach will not be forgotten.

Mr. Adams would stop by our house to talk business with Daddy at times when he was on his way to Corolla. He and my grandmother, Carrie Boswood (who was many years his senior), became great friends. The summer before Mr. Adams died, he sent a boat to Waterlily to carry Granny, who was 84 years old at the time, to Whalehead to have lunch with him. She enjoyed going there again since her two grandfathers, Abraham Baum and Samuel McHorney, had both owned much of this land through land grants from the state of North Carolina, dating back to 1830 (Morris, 2006).

The house and property were sold many times until 1992 when Currituck County bought the once-elegant home and what was left of the original land. Take time to visit this National Historic Site which is on the National Register of Historic Places. Tours are available year round from 9:00 a.m. – 5:00 p.m.

Contact the Whalehead Preservation Trust for more information. This organization can be reached at P.O. Box 307, Corolla, NC 27927, 252-453-9040 or visit them on the web at www.whaleheadclub.org.

Currituck Beach Lighthouse

Built in 1875, this lighthouse is the last lighthouse to be constructed on the Atlantic coast of North Carolina. It has the distinction of being the only light in North Carolina that is still housed in its original structure. The original Fresnel lens begins its lighted navigational service at dusk every day flashing on for 3 seconds and off for 17. The signal distance is 19 nautical miles. It is the most northern of the North Carolina lighthouses, located half way between its twin, Bodie Light to the south, and Cape Henry Light in Virginia Beach, Virginia to the north. While Bodie has been painted (as most lighthouses are and no two are painted

vs

alike), the red brick of the Currituck Beach Light has been left unpainted. It is a handsome structure of over one million bricks with the overall height of the tower at 163 feet with 214 steps to the top. Because of its height along a very flat section of the Atlantic coast, it is also visible while paddling from many places along the bays and sounds. Look south for it when paddling from Knotts Island to Carova or to the northeast when paddling from Poplar Branch Landing. It is the last lighthouse to be constructed on the coast of North Carolina.

Also known locally as the Corolla Light, the lighthouse is open for visitation from Good Friday to the weekend following Thanksgiving and offers a spectacular view not only of the Atlantic Ocean, but the Currituck Sound as well. The Light Keeper's House has been restored by the Outer Banks Conservationists, Inc., but is open only 12 days a year. For more information on the two structures, call 252-453-4939 or 252-453-8152.

View of the lighthouse
from the Whalehead Club

14

vs

Living at Corolla's Lighthouse

Norris Austin, a third generation Corolla man, relates his family's connection to Corolla and to the lighthouse compound:

The Austins got to Corolla because my grandfather [William Riley Austin] was the lighthouse keeper. He was in the Lighthouse Service and transferred here from Hatteras in 1891. Granddaddy served here until he retired in 1929.

There were three different houses at the lighthouse, and three keepers' families lived there all the time.

The Charleston Earthquake in 1886 cracked the lighthouse. The story is told the earthquake shook it so badly that Etta Dutton, a young woman was not able to walk down the steps, and slid all the way down with a baby in her arms.

Daddy [John Austin] said that his father liked to keep him busy with jobs when he was a boy. One of his jobs at the lighthouse was to clear the little brick walks around it of every blade of grass.

In the wintertime he had to carry off ducks and geese that were blinded and crashed into the light every night. There was a basket type netting around the top of the lighthouse to catch the piles of wildfowl. Sometimes whole flocks crashed into the light. Daddy carried the ducks and geese and gave them to the people in the neighborhood for food.

The lighthouse has watched folks come and go for over a century. I have always sensed an aura of mystery about Currituck Beach Light. It has seen sailing ships go past Corolla, planes in the sky flying over and helicopters transporting the sick to hospitals in Virginia. It has also experienced the howling winds of hurricanes and many, many northeasters, and has seen the perils of World War II.

My brother's children are the fourth generation of Austins who have slept under its warning beam of light.

~ Excerpt courtesy of Suzanne Tate, *Whalehead, Tales of Corolla*, N.C. 1987

We forget that the water cycle and the life cycle are one.

Jacques Cousteau

Paddling Sections

Section 1. (A) Poplar Branch Landing to Mossey Islands/ Brant Island, 3 miles, one way, (B) Whalehead, 6½ miles

From Poplar Branch Landing, paddle northeast to reach the Mossey Islands. A mile further puts the paddler at Brant Island and neighboring Thorofare Island. It is easy to become disoriented in these marsh areas, so a current marine chart is recommended as no road maps are accurate enough. Two miles to the north of Thorofare Island is the spit of land that marks Great Beach Pond.

These islands are all private properties and as such are named by the local fishermen who still refer to them by name to designate fishing areas. Some of the names are quite colorful, such as Rattlesnake Island, Cat Island, Bearhead, etc. This is private property and camping is not allowed.

Continuing to the northeast is Whalehead. This is a good spot to paddle into for birdwatching. Unless doubling back, this trip requires that a shuttle be run. The trip by land will take at least an hour, one way. This trip can be made longer if paddling through the islands near Sanders Bay.

Canada Geese

Brants

Wild Geese

Brant Island was most likely named for the brant goose, an arctic bird that winters on the Atlantic coast. Brants look very similar to their relative, the Canada goose but have a smaller, shorter neck and lack the conspicuous white cheek patch. Their favorite food is eelgrass which grows in shallow coastal waters. Due to a depletion of eelgrass in the early 1930s, brants turned to algae and widgeongrass, a submerged aquatic plant that grows in the bay and sound, for its food.

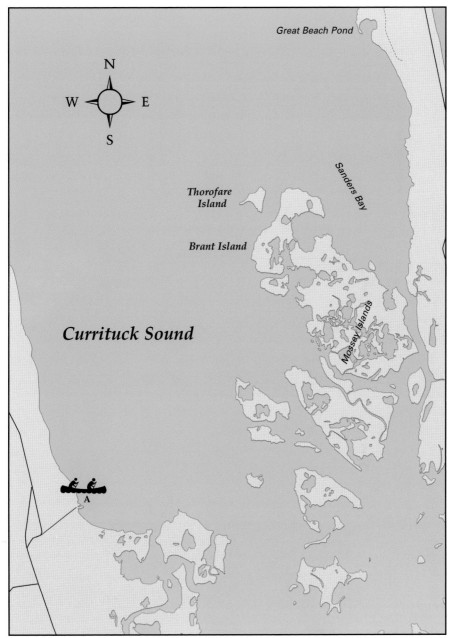

Great Beach Pond

N
W ✦ E
S

Thorofare Island

Sanders Bay

Brant Island

Currituck Sound

Mossey Islands

A

Map 3: Islands in Currituck Sound   © *Vickie Shufer*

Canada geese are more widespread than brants and are found in the lakes, bays, rivers and marshes bordering the Currituck Sound, Knotts Island and Back Bay areas. In some areas they have become semi-domesticated. They feed in open grasslands of marshes and even farm fields, and when food is available, have become year round residents.

A Duck Hunting Memory

A memory of duck hunting in the 1940s is written by Travis Morris.

When we got to Whalehead, it would be getting late in the afternoon and there would usually be a big bunch of Canvasback [ducks] out by the end of the point as we were headed in the channel to the club. Mr. Adams fed these ducks there and didn't shoot them; soon people could see them from the big picture window in the living room. When we got in the basin to the dock, somebody would be there with an old Army truck to take the bags up to the house; there was a command car for the guests to ride in.

When we got up to the house there were roaring oak fires in the fireplaces. After everybody got settled in their rooms, the men had drinks and it would soon be time for dinner. Afterward the men sat around to spin yarns until bedtime. By 8:30 p.m. Mr. Adams would tell his guests to stay up as long as they wanted to, but he was going to bed. During the night I was so excited anticipating the next day's hunt that I hardly slept. At about 5:00 a.m. somebody knocked on the door and told us it was time to get up. "We got up and went down to the dining room for a big breakfast. After breakfast we walked to the dock in front of the club. The guides had tied several skiffs behind each gas boat and dropped them off at various blinds. At lunchtime the gas boats came by to pick everybody up for lunch. After lunch and usually a nap, we went back out to hunt until take up time, at 4:20 p.m. I have seen as many as one hundred ducks and geese at the game room in the boat house (Morris, 2006).

Mallards *vs*

Aerial view of Whalehead Club and vicinity   *vs*

Outer Banks Center for Wildlife Education

The Outer Banks Center for Wildlife Education, a new education center of the NC Wildlife Commission, is located in the Currituck Heritage Park in Corolla, NC and opened in 2005. This facility is among the three such centers located in North Carolina. Others are in Pisgah Forest and Raleigh, North Carolina.

The Outer Banks Wildlife Education Center offers special programs on plants and animals including educational kayak trips available to the public. For complete information contact the Program Coordinator at P.O. Box 502, Corolla, NC 27927, 252-453-0221 or visit the web site at www.ncwildlife.org.

Outer Banks Center for Wildlife Education   *Photo by Mark Buckler*
                                                    Outer Banks Center for Wildlife Education

19

Section 2. (B) Whalehead Club to Monkey Island, 3 miles one way

Paddling north from the launch site, the paddler will notice what appears to be two small islands about 1 mile from the launching area. This is Jones Point. At high water, it is possible to paddle between them. Otherwise, go to the left around the island. Just north of the island is Raccoon Bay.

On a clear day Mary's Island can be spotted, about 1 mile northwest of Jones Point. Mary's Island is narrow and only about ½ mile long. Mostly a sandbar, it provides a resting for shorebirds, including seagulls, terns and oystercatchers.

Beyond Mary's Island, about 1 mile to the north, is Monkey Island. Paddling to Monkey Island is an experience in itself. Monkey Island tract as well as several other small islands are a part of the Currituck National Wildlife Refuge and managed by the U.S. Fish and Wildlife Service. As such, it is protected from disturbance and has become an extraordinary bird sanctuary. Wading birds, including herons, egrets and ibis are colonial nesting birds and have developed a rookery on the island, using the tall pine trees as nesting sites. Many birds can be observed in flight while going back and forth between their feeding and nesting grounds. Osprey also build their large nests of branches and twigs at the tops of tall trees while neotropical songbirds nest in the understory. Waterfowl abound during the winter months. There are signs on Monkey Island advising that this is not a place to land. Even though there is no take-out at this island, you can quietly circle around the island from a distance and observe great egrets, little blue herons, great blue herons, glossy ibis, osprey and numerous other bird species that use this island as a nesting site.

From Monkey Island, the paddler can go east to Jenkins Cove. All of the shoreline for about two miles is part of the refuge holdings. Please honor the refuge's mission of protecting the land and its wildlife. Paddling the return trip south along the shoreline will offer plenty of bird-watching opportunities as well as protection from strong winds.

Monkey Island

vs

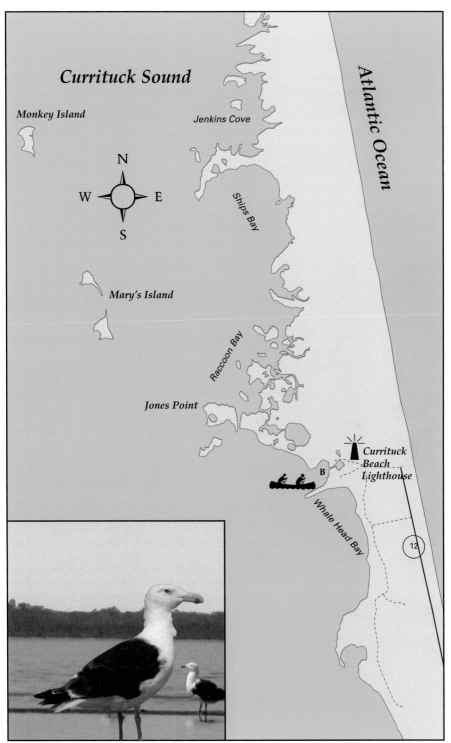

Currituck Sound

Monkey Island

Jenkins Cove

Atlantic Ocean

N
W   E
S

Ships Bay

Mary's Island

Raccoon Bay

Jones Point

Currituck
Beach
Lighthouse

B

Whale Head Bay

12

Greater Black-backed Gull   **Map 4:** Whalehead to Monkey Island   © *Vickie Shufer*

21

Monkey Island

Standing at the rail atop the Currituck Light, the coast line of the Currituck Banks including the building boom that was once the small village of Corolla can be seen. Looking northwest to soundward, there is only one visible island with trees: Monkey Island.

It contains no monkeys, but abounds with birdlife. It is the largest heron rookery in the North Carolina Outer Banks currently supporting three types of herons: the great blue heron, little blue heron and tri-colored heron. According to the U.S. Fish and Wildlife Service website, in the early 1980s land began to be acquired that would by 1984 establish the Currituck National Wildlife Refuge. Monkey Island's history is listed briefly as a former home of the Pamunkey Indians, hence its name. Indian artifacts have been found there, continues the narrative, suggesting that these Indians were expert fishermen. Are these the same Pamunkey Indians of the Pamunkey tribe which today is centered on the Pamunkey River northeast of the James River? Whoever these early Americans were, it may be assumed that the hunting on Monkey Island was good, whether fish or fowl was prey.

An interesting study of old Currituck Sound maps dating from 1672 to 1882 all show islands which may be Monkey Island. The earliest map naming Monkey Island that the authors have found thus far is the 1770 map made by the engraver I. Bagly for Captain Collet. This map clearly shows Monkey Island to be one of only four named islands (besides Knotts Island which appears as a peninsula connected by marsh to the mainland) in Currituck Sound. The Ogilby map of 1672 shows four large islands in Currituck Sound, one of which is probably Monkey. By 1733, the same large island still existed located just about where the supposed Monkey Island was on the 1672 map. A Civil War map of 1865 has Monkey still visible, though not named. By 1882, there is an entire cluster of islands drawn where Monkey should be. Apparently, Monkey Island has eroded or dwindled in size through the years. This island may have been much larger if the maps are to be believed.

Monkey Island Hunt Club

A weathered, dilapidated building hidden among the trees, with a decaying bulkhead in front is all that is left of what was once a prominent hunt club on Monkey Island. In 1919, a lodge was built for a private waterfowl hunt club called the Monkey Island Club. Outbuildings were built and the lodge had a unique position in Currituck Sound as being approachable only by boat. In the 1930s it was owned by the Penn family from Reidsville, North Carolina who was very successful in the railroad business and enjoyed coming to Currituck Sound to hunt and fish. After becoming lost in the fog on one hunting trip, Mr. Penn had a bell delivered from an old locomotive so the caretaker could signal to them if they did not show up at the scheduled time. Since that time the bell has been moved to the grounds of the Whalehead Club where it can be viewed today by visitors. The bell was donated by Levie C. Bunch, Jr. in memory of his grandfather

Great Egret *vs*

Aerial view of Monkey Island showing erosion
as evidenced by old bulkhead boundary

Photo by Drew C. Wilson /
The Virginian-Pilot

Horace J. Barnett, who worked at the Whalehead Club.

The last private owner in 1974 opened the club to the public. Later The Nature Conservancy bought Monkey Island along with a section of barrier island along the Currituck Banks. The land was transferred in 1981 to the U.S. Fish and Wildlife Service. Today the trees serve as roosts and nesting sites for herons, egrets, ibis, osprey and other marsh birds.

Above is an aerial photo of Monkey Island today showing the old lodge and the outbuildings. Notice the old boundary of the island marked by the old bulkhead. The island is still shrinking as erosion takes its toll. The causes of erosion are being investigated by several groups that are trying to save this historic site.

Currituck Sound – a low salt Estuary

Currituck Sound is a low salt estuary which supports a variety of aquatic life, including blue-spotted sunfish, bluegill, yellow perch, silversides, pumpkinseed, channel catfish, shad, herring, carp and eels. Because the sound is a low salinity estuary, certain fresh and saltwater species can live here together.

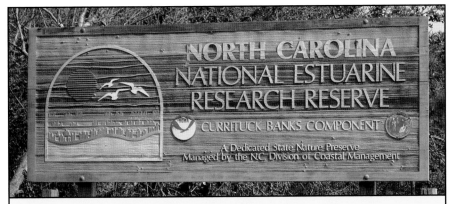

North Carolina National Estuarine Research Reserve

In 1989, the North Carolina General Assembly authorized the establishment of the North Carolina Coastal Reserve Program. Through this scientific program, unique coastal sites are to be protected. A part of this ten site system includes four unique areas collectively known as the North Carolina National Estuarine Research Reserve. These four sites include Currituck Banks, Rachel Carson, Masonboro Island, and Zeke's Island. In the scope of this book is the Currituck Banks section. Managing the Currituck Banks is the NC Division of Coastal Management in partnership with the National Oceanic and Atmospheric Administration under the Coastal Zone Management Act (www.ncneer.org, 2005).

The living laboratory of Currituck Banks ranges from the sand dunes of the Atlantic north of Corolla, across to Ships Bay to a tiny island north of Mary's Islands, then south just to the east of Mary's Islands in Currituck Sound. The border then crosses back to the Atlantic taking a zig-zag course northeast of Raccoon Bay. The 954 acre site is bordered by properties belonging to The Nature Conservancy and the U.S. Fish and Wildlife Service. Appearing wild and wind-blown, this is truly Currituck's "Outback."

This barrier island habitat is open to the public. A public parking lot is located ¾ mile north of the village of Corolla. From the parking area follow the ⅓ mile boardwalk trail through a maritime forest of live oaks and loblolly pines with highbush blueberries, serviceberries and waxmyrtles in the understory. The boardwalk trail leads to a marsh area lined with rushes at the edge of Currituck Sound. If the tide is out look for tracks in the mud flats where otter, raccoon, deer and other wildlife visit each day.

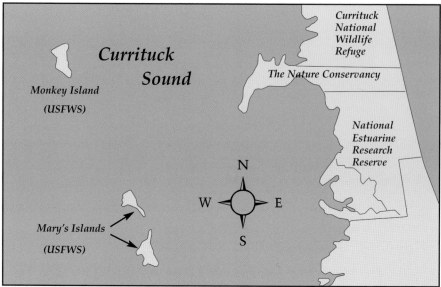

Map 5: National Estuarine Research Reserve, The Nature Conservancy
and the Currituck National Wildlife Refuge

© Vickie Shufer

About halfway down the boardwalk trail there is a 1½ mile round-trip primitive trail that winds through a magnificent maritime forest and emerges at Currituck Sound north of the boardwalk trail. At low tide it is possible to walk along the sandy beach. Stunning sunset views can be observed looking west across the sound.

For information, call North Carolina Coastal Reserve, 252-261-8891.

Hiking trail at North Carolina Coastal Reserve

vs

Currituck National Wildlife Refuge

Located ¾ of a mile north of Corolla is the Currituck National Wildlife Refuge. The refuge consists of five main tracts that encompass 4,110 acres of wetlands, woodlands, brush and beach. The area is managed as a satellite of Mackay Island National Wildlife Refuge. During the summer months there are large concentrations of wading birds, shorebirds, raptors as well as a variety of mammals, reptiles and amphibians. Piping plovers and loggerhead sea turtles occasionally nest on the beach. During the winter months the refuge is host to waterfowl and other migratory birds.

For more information call 252-429-3100 or visit http://mackay island.fws.gov/currituck.

Currituck Inlet and Shifting Sands

The first recorded inlet into Currituck Sound is reported as opening in 1657. This is probably the same cut or inlet in the coastline of North Carolina on a map dated about 1685 and marked at 36 degrees 30 minutes. It was labeled as "Caratuck." In 1728, William Byrd records that inlet as the "old" Currituck Inlet and he describes seeing a sloop in the sound that had entered thorough the "new" Currituck Inlet. This new inlet had opened during a hurricane on September 17, 1713 (NOAA, 2001). He mentions that ships having no greater than ten-foot draft could pass through it. His group went to the old inlet, the original measuring point for the boundary line between the colonies of Virginia and North Carolina. Barely an inlet at this period in history, Byrd described it as "an Opening of not quite a Mile, which at this day is not practicable for any Vessel whatsoever. And as shallow as it now is, it continues to fill up more and more, both the Wind and Waves rolling in the Sands from the Eastern Shoals" (Byrd, 1728). The new inlet was about five miles from the old inlet. The new inlet closed completely before the mid 1800's.

A report in the *Pennsylvania Gazette* from October 5, 1785 reports a violent storm that occurred in late September concerning the sloop, *Delaware*, arriving from Turk's Island having lost her mast and every-thing on deck. "They went ashore at Currituck, to get supplies, but the gale had been so severe there, that the sea had made a breach into the Sound and laid the country under water for two or three miles, washed

Migrating dunes

away many houses, together with almost all their cattle and ground stock; many of the inhabitants were obliged to secure themselves in trees, several lives were lost, and the shore for some miles was covered with drowned cattle, household goods, &c."

Other coastal storms have opened the sound to the ocean, like Caffeys Inlet in 1790, but the cuts closed quickly. As many as twenty-six former inlets along the Outer Banks have been significant to have had their names included on navigational charts (Kaufman and Pilkey, 1979). Today, there are no inlets from Currituck Sound to the Atlantic Ocean (Reprinted from *Wild River Guide to Dismal Swamp Water Trails* by Gilbert and Shufer).

The Currituck Banks and the entire Outer Banks of North Carolina are constantly on the move. As recently as the Ash Wednesday storm of 1962, salt water washed over the dunes and destroyed the last village at Penny's Hill (Kaufman and Pilkey, 1979). The former fishing village of Sea Gull, north of present Corolla, North Carolina, contained a school, thirty-five houses, two churches and a post office (Tennant, 2001). The tallest sand dune on the East Coast, Penny's Hill, has buried at least one small community. A bit farther south along the U.S. 158 Bypass/Virginia Dare Boulevard at Jockeys Ridge sand dune in Nags Head, NC, the casual visitor today will notice the small castle being unearthed by the shifting sand. This is the remnant of a miniature golf establishment that has been buried and is now visible due to another phase of the sand's movements. Tomorrow, who knows? What is certain is that the dunes and the Outer Banks will continue to move.

Wild Horses

Horses are not native to the North American continent. It is with wonder and excitement that a visitor to the Currituck Banks spots his or her first wild horse. To see these horses from the vantage point of a kayak is certainly a unique experience, one that is not forgotten. While being used to people on foot or in an automobile, a quiet, slow-moving boater is still a fairly new experience for the horses.

It is estimated that the wild horses of the Currituck Banks, also known as Spanish mustangs, may have blood lines going back as far as four centuries. These horses are thought by some to have come from descendants of intentional beaching by Spanish explorers or shipwrecks from which the horses swam to shore. They appear to be related to the Spanish barb, a horse originally from the Barbary Coast of Africa. The Spanish preferred this sturdy, small breed and these characteristics may have made these tough horses perfect for traveling by ship. After all, a smaller animal requires less food and the rugged sea voyages certainly demanded sturdiness. In a blood typing study conducted at the University of Kentucky, it was stated by E. Gus Cothran, PhD that "in terms of genetic marker makeup, the Corolla wild horses are absolutely unique." And, "… from a comparative aspect, the Corolla herd is far more like horse breeds of clear Spanish origins than any other group of horses …" (CWHF, 2004). Whatever their origin, the wild Banks' ponies provide a provocative look at the past.

The continuing story of the survival of this hearty breed of small horses is kept alive by the Corolla Wild Horse Fund, Inc. Formed in 1989, this non-profit group of concerned citizens began their cause of protecting and preserving this valuable beach heritage. The beautiful beach horses are wild and it is one of the goals of the CWHF to keep them so. A management plan adopted by Currituck County in March 2000 was also adopted by the Outer Banks Conservationists Inc., The North Carolina National Estuarine Research Reserve, the Department of Environmental and Natural Resources, and the Currituck National Wildlife Refuge, U.S.

Department of the Interior. The Corolla County Ordinance is listed under "Animals: Article II. Wild Horses, Sec.3-31, Luring, enticing, seizing; states it shall further be unlawful for any person to lure, attract, or entice a wild horse to come within 50 feet of any person."

As interesting and as alluring as these animals are, beachgoers are advised that because these horses are wild, their behavior can be unpredictable. Admire from afar and do not try to approach or feed these beautiful residents. For more information, contact Corolla Wild Horse Fund, Inc. at PO Box 361, Corolla, NC 27927; telephone: 252-453-8002; or on the web at www.corollawildhorses.com.

Wild Horses   *vs*

Part 2

Knotts Island Bay

Knotts Island Bay

Knotts Island Bay separates the "Island" from the Outer Banks of North Carolina and at its widest point is just under 2 miles. It connects to the waters of Back Bay to the north via the Knotts Island Channel, a distance of just around 3 miles.

The water of Knotts Island Bay is colored dark by tree tannins and today is probably more fresh than brackish. Underwater grasses seem to be making a comeback and waterfowl are frequent visitors. One never knows what may be found exploring the various small channels. On one of our recent paddling trips we found part of an old duck decoy. Shorebirds are commonly seen along the grassy banks, so take binoculars and see how many different birds you can spot. While paddling here, also look for the Currituck Beach Lighthouse, about 9 miles to the south. See page 14 for a description of this famous lighthouse.

Location

Just south of Virginia Beach, Virginia, Knotts Island Bay is nestled between Knotts Island and Currituck Banks. It is the link between the Currituck Sound to the south and Back Bay to the north. The state line between North Carolina and Virginia slices through the northern end of Knotts Island and is the dividing line between Currituck Banks and False Cape State Park.

Access Point

A. NC Wildlife Resources Commission Boat Ramp – SR 1259/ Brumley Road

B. Bay Villa Marina

C. Mackay Island Road

Boat Ramp at Bay Villa Marina

vs

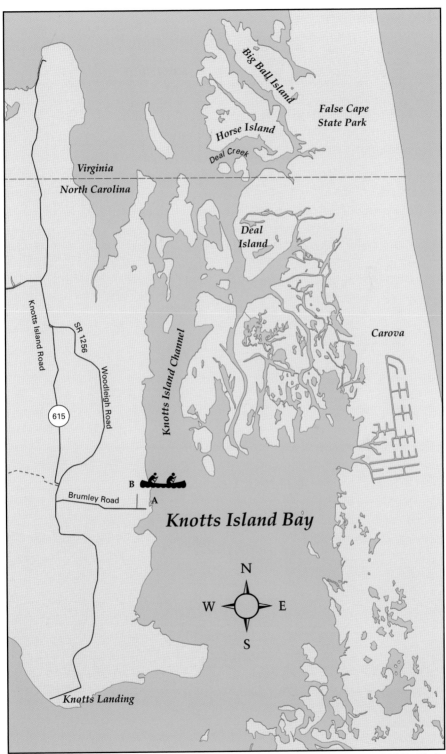

Map 6: Knotts Island Bay

© Vickie Shufer

Access Points
A. NC Wildlife Resources Commission Boat Ramp, SR 1259/Brumley Road

Directions: From Virginia Beach, Virginia follow NC Route 615/Princess Anne Road south across the Marsh Causeway to Knotts Island. Stay on NC Route 615 and go south at the curve in the road at the Knotts Island United Methodist Church approximately 2 miles. Continue south until you reach SR 1259/Brumley Road. Turn east and follow the paved road almost 1 mile to its end. There is a narrow sandy beach from which to launch a canoe or kayak. A large parking lot is located less than ⅒ of a mile west of the launch site. This is usually an uncrowded site, so it is possible to off-load kayaks and gear, then go park and walk back to the put-in. There are no facilities here but about ½ mile west of the parking lot is the Knotts Island Ruritan Park with picnic shelters and restrooms. It is open daily from 8:00 a.m. to sunset.

From North Carolina, take NC Route 158 toward Barco and drive on NC Route 168 north to the Currituck/Knotts Island Ferry in Currituck County. The crossing time over Currituck Sound/North Landing is 45 minutes. This can be a highlight of one's day and offers a grand view of the Intracoastal Waterway here. The 18-car Currituck/Knotts Island Ferry is free and runs year-round, six times a day, weather permitting. The ferry ride ends at the southern end of Knotts Island. Take NC Route 615 north to the access sites. For information on this particular ferry, call 252-232-2683.

Brumley Road launch site

vs

B. Bay Villa Marina

Directions: Follow the directions for Access Point A to Brumley Road. Go east on Brumley Road to Bay Villa Lane, just before the boat ramp, and turn north. Go to the end of the gravel road to Bay Villa Marina and Restaurant. There is a $5 launching fee for motorboats; canoes and kayaks are free. The restaurant offers family dining in the evening. Call 252-429-3559 for hours and specials.

C. Mackay Island Road

Directions: After crossing the Marsh Causeway to Knotts Island, stay on NC Route 615 and go south at the curve in the road at the Knotts Island United Methodist Church. Look for the entrance to Mackay Island National Wildlife Refuge on the west (right) side of NC Route 615. Follow the entrance road to Mackay Island Road and turn west (right). Go a short distance until you see a sign on the north (right) side of Mackay Island Road and a launching area near the dike gate. The parking area is just past the launch site on the south (left) side of Mackay Island Road.

Closures: From October 16 through March 14, boats are not allowed and most of the refuge is closed for public access to reduce disturbance to wintering waterfowl. Mackay Island Road from NC Route 615 to the dike road, the Great Marsh Loop Trail, the Kurault Trail Overlook and the Marsh Causeway are open year round. Additional closures may occur periodically for various reasons. Call the refuge office at 252-429-3100 for up-to-date information or visit http://mackayisland.fws.gov.

Camping: Three private campgrounds are nearby: **Barnes Campground**, located at 108 Barnes Lane, (252) 429-3163; **Sandy Point Resort Campground**, 176 Sandy Point Drive, (252) 429-3094; and the **North Landing Beach Riverfront Campground and Resort**, 161 Princess Anne Rd, Virginia Beach, VA 23456, 757-426-6241.

Mackay Island Road launch site   *vs*

The North Carolina Ferry Division

The original motorized ferries were privately owned and began operating in the 1920's. The state of North Carolina began subsidizing these services in 1934 and established the North Carolina Ferry Division (of the North Carolina Department of Transportation) in 1947. Today, the North Carolina Ferry Division has seven routes and operates 24 ferry vessels, several support vessels, and a dredge to keep access open. The ferries are quite versatile operating in as little as five feet of water and allowing almost any type of motor vehicle. Every North Carolina ferry route connects to a bicycling highway. Three of the ferry routes operate year-round and there is no fee for these particular crossing services. In fact, most of the ferries are cost-free. Reservations are required when leaving Cedar Island, Orcacoke, and Swan Quarter.

To get to the Knotts Island Ferry from Virginia Beach, Virginia, follow VA Route 615/Princess Anne Road, crossing the North Carolina border. The route number is the same, but the highway is now NC Route 615. Continue south to the end of NC Route 615 on Knotts Island and follow signs to the ferry site. This ferry is free and crosses the North Landing River to Currituck, North Carolina. Call 800-BY FERRY for schedule and complete information.

Paddling Sections

Section 1. (A) Knotts Island to Carova Beach – 2¹/₂ miles, one way.

A favorite paddling trip of the authors is to put in at Knotts Island, paddle over to Carova Beach, walk over to the Atlantic Ocean, have a picnic and swim, then return to the relatively fresh water of Knotts Island Bay.

From the launch site at the end of SR 1259/Brumley Road, paddle due east across the Knotts Island Channel and enter the northern end of Knotts Island Bay. The water is mostly shallow outside of the channel. On the way to Carova, while paddling across the northern end of the shallow Knotts Island Bay, look to the south for the Currituck Beach Lighthouse. Although it is 9½ miles away, this lighthouse is visible on a clear day and is in the village of Corolla, North Carolina. It is also known locally as the Corolla Light. For lighthouse information, see page 14.

To get to the Atlantic beach at Carova, we follow the larger canals and usually manage to find the Carova Fire Station to purchase some ice cream or a cold drink in warm weather and a hot drink in cooler weather. The folks there are very friendly and are very knowledgeable about the history and ecology of the area. We request permission to stow our boats nearby and then walk the short hike to the beach. Four–wheel drive vehicles are allowed on the beach and we find the shoulder seasons more relaxing than the busy summer weekends. However even in summer, the rugged beach and high dune backdrop remind one of earlier times.

On the paddler's return trip, a dip in the low salinity waters of the Knotts Island Bay is a way to wash off the salt from a swim in the Atlantic Ocean. Paddle back to the launch site and consider a driving trip to the local vineyards and pick-your-own orchards. See page 39.

Paddling Tip

When paddling across Knotts Island Bay a chart and compass are not really necessary, but might be useful for one's first trip. In fog, a compass or GPS adds a terrific sense of security.

Beach Treasures

On the sands we saw Conque-Shells in great Number of which the Indians make both their Blue and white Peak, both colours being in different Parts of the same Shell (Byrd, 1728).

Seashells and other beach artifacts dot the coastline as they are deposited by the incoming tides each day. If time allows, walk north from Carova Beach toward the more pristine beach of False Cape State Park on the Virginia side to find an abundance of beach treasures.

Sea Snails

The "Conque-Shells" that Byrd wrote about are actually whelks, a marine sea snail with a spiral-shaped shell that is frequently found along the coast. The string of cylindrical discs is the egg case and contains hundreds of immature whelks, exact replicas of the parent. Most sea snails are predators and prey on bivalves.

Whelk egg case

Knobbed Whelk
vs

Moon snails have a smooth, globe-shaped shell and an enormous foot that they use to wrap around a clam while using their radula to drill a hole into the shell of the clam. They are then able to slowly extract the contents.

vs

Moon Snail

Limpets are also snails but they have a tent-shaped shell rather than a spiral shell. They attach themselves to rocks or other firm objects.

vs

Limpet

Bivalves

Most of the shells found on the beach are bivalves. The soft-bodied animal that lives within has a hatchet-shaped foot adapted for burrowing. Bivalves are filter feeders, using tubular siphons to bring water, along with food particles, into their systems.

Scallop

vs

Angel Wing

Echinoderms

Echinoderms are spiny-skinned animals that are bottom feeders or reef-dwellers. A five-rayed pattern is displayed on the body of each.

vs

Sand Dollar

Sea Star

Orchards and Vineyards

Early English explorers of the Outer Banks and Inner Banks of what was to be called North Carolina remarked often about the native rich plant life, particularly the grapes. In 1584 while exploring for Sir Walter Raleigh, the sea captains Phillip

Photo Courtesy of Martin Vineyards

Amadas and Arthur Barlowe wrote that the coast of North Carolina was "...so full of grapes as the very beating and surge of the sea overflowed them...in all the world, the like abundance is not to be found." The grapes they had discovered were probably muscadines, the ancestors of today's cultivated muscadine.

The grape growing heritage of the land is a delight to today's coastal explorer. While in the area, be sure to make a stop at Martin's Orchard to pick peaches, apples, pumpkins, or other seasonal fruit. Martin Vineyard is on the same property so pay a visit to this waterfront winery. A second winery just to the north is Moonrise Bay Vineyard. Both of these establishments have wine tastings and picnic tables. This is a very special part of this unique paddling day. Both vineyards are right on the water. If the lunchtime paddling trip didn't include lunch on the beach at Carova, do plan a picnic stop at either of the vineyards. Bring your own food and water. They have portable restrooms and vending machines for cold drinks. They don't mind if you show up in your paddling clothes. Adults may wish to sample some of the wines made on the estate. Do call ahead to be sure they will be open.

To reach these vineyards and orchards by land, take Route 615 across the Marsh Causeway to Knotts Island until the curve in the road at the Knotts Island United Methodist Church. Follow NC SR 1256/ Woodleigh Road that goes to the east of the church. There are signs directing you to both Martin's and Moonrise Bay. The driving distance from one to the other is less than a mile. Both are easy to find and well worth the trip.

Additional Information

Martin Vineyards and Martin's Orchards, 213 Martin Farm Lane, Knotts Island, NC, 27950. Phone (252) 429-3542; www.martinvineyards.com.
Moonrise Bay Vineyard, 134 Moonrise Bay Landing, Knotts Island, NC, 27950. Phone (252) 429-9463; www.moonrisebaywine.com.
All North Carolina Vineyards: www.ncwine.org.

Section 2. Knotts Island to Deal Island – 2 miles, one way.

This is a trip to the lower section of marshlands that connect to False Cape State Park in Virginia. From the launch site at the end of Bay Villa Lane, head north through the Knotts Island Channel. In a little over a mile, turn at the first large opening to the east. Follow this to the end and paddle north where a small channel may be visible. At times this is not navigable. Deal Island is private property, so getting out of one's boat is not permitted. Take time on the return route to explore some of the islands and smaller waterways that connect to Knotts Island Bay. The paddler may make this a loop trip, returning through the small eastern channel that parallels Knotts Island Channel.

The Deal Island Shooting Club was chartered in 1891. The clubhouse was built on the North Carolina side of Deal Island. Ownership changed in 1905 and again in 1915 when the club was changed to Deal Island Ducking Club, Inc. Pictured below is an outbuilding once belonging to the club.

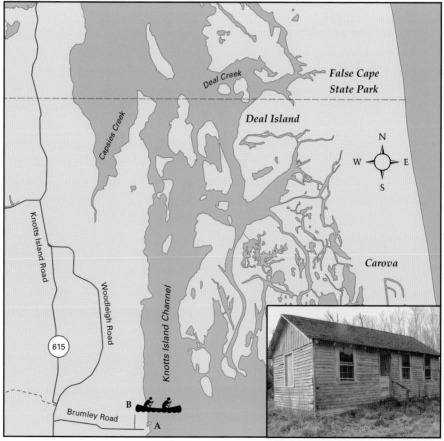

Map 7: Knotts Island to Deal Island

Outbuilding from the Deal Island Club

Collection of Lillie Gilbert

Yaupon Holly (Japon Tea)

At Currituck Beach in 1728, the survey party of William Byrd II with a "Cedar-Post to be driven deep into the Sand" (Byrd, 1728) pronounced the boundary of North Carolina and Virginia. Besides the cedar trees that grew in abundance along the higher ground of the Currituck Beach, Byrd also describes other plants of interest: "Among the Shrubs, we were shewed here and there a Bush of Carolina-Tea, called Japon ... This is an Evergreen, the Leaves whereof have some resemblance to Tea, but differ very widely both in Tast and Flavour" (Byrd, 1728). According to John Lawson, another early writer, "all of the coastal Carolina Indians made a tea from the yaupon tree" (Hudson, 1979). Moses Curtis described in *The Trees of North Carolina*, 1883, a ceremony in which inland groups of American Indians made an annual pilgrimage to the coast where they prepared a black drink from the yaupon leaves which they used as an emetic and would drink for two or three days until they were purged and would then return home, each taking a bundle of yaupon with them.

Yaupon tea, although not served as a purgative, became a customary breakfast drink in the Carolinas according to a report by a German traveler, Johann David Schöpf, who visited North Carolina in 1783 and 1784. Every farmer on Knotts Island was said to have a "patch of yaupon in his yard and puts up a barrel or so of it every year" (Hudson, 1979). Local use continued into the twentieth century and became popular at Nags Head resorts. It was recognized as a traditional local specialty and was reported as recently as 1973 to be served at the **Pony Island Restaurant** on Ocracoke Island. Today you can purchase bags of dried leaves at the **Ocracoke Preservation Museum** at the end of Ocracoke Island. This was a cash crop for many "Bankers" who sold yaupon tea to people on the mainland. "Even as late as World War II, the Bankers found outside markets for seaweed and Yaupon" (Barfield, 1995).

Yaupon is a large evergreen shrub or small tree, often forming thickets in southeastern coastal areas. It blooms in the spring with numerous tiny white fragrant flowers. These are followed by shiny red berries that mature in autumn and often remain attached throughout the winter, making a popular holiday decoration. Even though the berries may be toxic to humans, fruit-eating birds feed on them during the winter months when other fruits are scarce.

Section 3. (C) Mackay Island Road to canals – mileage variable

Paddling in the canals in the wildlife refuge and the shallow bays off the causeway is fun if the wind has not been blowing hard. In some circumstances, like other parts of Back Bay, the water can literally be blown away leaving little or no water in which to paddle. A great time to paddle is in late summer or early fall when the mallows are in full bloom. This area is beautiful with flowering plants. Watch overhead for eagles, osprey or various hawks. A chart, map, compass or GPS may be helpful if you venture into the canals. It all starts looking alike and it's easy to lose one's way. If a paddler does get "lost," it's possible to listen for cars on the road and try to walk out. Be aware that if trying to walk in the marsh areas, that what looks like solid ground may not be after all. As William Byrd II said of his surveyors paddling here in 1728 as part of the state line team:

> They carried the Line thro' the firm land of Knot's Island, where it was no more than half a mile wide. After they travers'd a large marsh, that was exceeding Miry, and extended to an arm of the Back-Bay. They crosst that in a canoe, which we had ordered round for that Purpose, and then waded over another Marsh, that reached quite to the High Land of Princess Anne. Both these Marshes together make a breadth of five Miles, in which the Men frequently sunk up to the Middle without muttering the least complaint.

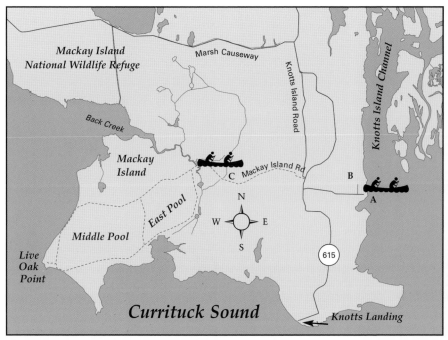

Map 8: Mackay Island Canals and Causeway

© Vickie Shufer

Lillie picking peaches   *Photo by Pati Terry*

Knotts Island

Knotts Island has been an agricultural community for generations. The rich sandy soil drains well and the mild climate is friendly to the growing of many diverse crops. Cool breezes blow from the Atlantic Ocean, which is as close as a mile and a half to Knotts Island's eastern shoreline. The former community of Fruitville was located here and one of the current local vineyards has paid tribute to the past by naming one of its wines "Fruitville Red." In honor of its most popular fruit, the community of Knotts Island sponsors the Peach Festival yearly at the end of July. Activities include a parade, live music at the Community Park, arts and crafts display and sale, and other local entertainment options that vary yearly.

Honoring both land and water is the Annual Wildlife Show which is held on the second weekend in October. With Mackay Island National Wildlife Refuge adjacent to Knotts Island proper, and so much water to paddle, a wildlife show is very appropriate to this community. Artists and crafts persons such as decoy carvers, outdoor photographers, sculptors and painters display their works. The local Ruritan Club provides Carolina Barbeque and other food to the attendees. For the latest information on the festivals, contact ruritanclub@knottsislandonline.com.

Hunt clubs have existed on both the Carolina and Virginia side of Knotts Island for over a century. The 75 acre Knotts Island Gunning Club was located on the Virginia end of the island and was founded by several hunters from Norfolk, Virginia. It ceased to exist after 1926 when its charter was dissolved.

Knotts Island History

While the English may claim to have discovered Knotts Island, American Indians lived there at least 600 years before the English arrived. It is said that in 1594, Captain James Knotts named the area for himself after sailing to it through a cut in the coastline of North Carolina. The cut or inlet is marked at 36 degrees 30 minutes as "Caratuck" on a map dated about 1685. The 1657 map of Comberford indicates "Knot Ile" and by 1685 a map showed the spelling as "Knotts Island." Settlers who later moved into the area were blessed with productive salt marshes, large oyster beds, and fish such as mullet and flounder. The "old" inlet at 36 degrees 30 minutes was almost closed by 1728 when William Byrd wrote about it in his diary. Byrd also mentions discovering that the island is actually a peninsula and predicted the success that landowners of the future might have by ditching and draining the land.

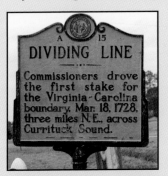

It was discover'd, by this day's Work, that Knot's Island was improperly so call'd, being in Truth no more than a Peninsula. The NW Side of it is only divided from the Main by a great Marsh ... which is seldom totally overfow'd. Instead of that, it might, by the Labour of a few Trenches, be drained into firm Meadow, capable of grazing as many cattle as Job, in his best Estate, was master of. In the Miry Condition it now lies, it feeds great Numbers in the Winter, tho', when the Weather grows warm, they are driven from thence by the Mighty Armies of Mosquetas, which are the Plague of the lower Part of Carolina...

William Byrd II, 1728

Knotts Island was a busy coastal community connected to the Atlantic Ocean by another inlet which opened in 1713. This was appropriately known as "New Currituck Inlet." Then came the hurricane of 1828. During this violent storm, the "new" Currituck Inlet was almost completely closed by coastal sand shifts. After the storm, the ecology changed dramatically as the saltwater bays and sounds became freshwater areas. By 1837, there was no trace of the "new inlet." The fishing was gone; the oysters died. Knotts Islanders struggled to rebuild their lives. Slowly, freshwater grasses appeared and the marsh areas grew to attract migratory ducks and geese. The new industry of wildfowl hunting and gunning also grew. Freshwater fish could be harvested and shipped via the North Landing River to the port of Norfolk.

Things were looking up for the locals until another coastal storm blew in from the northeast in March of 1846. The winds blew for two nights and one day, then three inches of snow fell. The fresh waters around Knotts Island and the Great Marsh Bay, which separated the community from the mainland of Currituck County, were inundated with salt water that was blown in over the dunes. This flooding killed the freshwater grasses and fouled the water for fishing. The next disaster happened that same year in September and this powerful hurricane is best remembered today as the one that opened Hatteras and Oregon Inlets (Cecelski, 2000). Today, with the established communities, greenery, forests and extensive marshes of Knotts Island, it is hard to imagine the hardships endured by the earlier inhabitants.

Knotts Island United Methodist Church

On the main highway, NC Route 616/Knotts Island Road is the principal landmark of old Knotts Island. This church was first established in 1811. The present frame structure was built by the congregation in 1902. The well-kept church is marked by a corner enclosed tower and broad gables that enclose the sanctuary. There is a cemetery on the property. For additional information, contact the church at 675 Knotts Island Road, Knotts Island, NC, 27950. Phone 252-429-3544.

vs

Mackay Island National Wildlife Refuge

Mackay Island National Wildlife Refuge, located in northeastern North Carolina with 874 acres in southeastern Virginia, consists of 8,138 acres of marsh, timberland and cropland. It was established in 1960 as a sanctuary for migratory waterfowl and in the fall and winter thousands of ducks, geese and swans flock to the refuge. During the summer months wading birds, several types of rails, osprey and bald eagles can be spotted. In addition to the bird life, there are also muskrat, nutria, river otter, raccoon, fox and whitetail deer that are permanent residents in the refuge.

Parts of the refuge and the refuge office are open to the public year round, including the Great Marsh Trail, the Kuralt Trail Overlook and the Marsh Causeway. However, most of the refuge is closed from October 16 through March 14 to reduce disturbance to wintering waterfowl. Periodically throughout the year, the refuge will hold an "Open Roads Day" in which visitors are permitted to drive on dike roads to observe wildlife. Other wildlife-dependent recreational opportunities are available at certain times and places on the refuge throughout the year and include wildlife observation, wildlife interpretation, photography, environmental education, fishing and hunting.

New to the causeway in 1999 was the observation platform over-looking the bay and marsh to the north of Mackay Island. This is part of the Charles Kuralt Trail. There are two sighting scopes for bird watchers on the platform. This is an excellent birding area for winter migratories. Notable among the thousands of wintering birds are the huge flocks of swans, Canada Geese and Snow Geese. Many varieties of ducks winter here as well as cormorants and coots.

The Marsh Causeway canals are accessible for small boats and launching is permitted from March 15 through October 15, sunrise to sunset. There is a designated canoe/kayak launch on Mackay Island Road (see p. 35). Note that the impoundments are closed to paddlers or any type of boat.

For more information contact the refuge at 252-429-3100 or visit them at www.fws.gov/mackayisland.

Tundra Swans vs

Migratory Birds

In the fall large numbers of migrating birds begin their journey south to their wintering grounds along the Atlantic Flyway. More than one million waterfowl and marsh birds will stop in Back Bay, Knotts Island Bay and Currituck Sound to feed and rest before moving on. An abundance of marsh grasses, seeds, tubers and other aquatic plants provides food for the waterfowl, whereas in northern climates ponds and lakes are frozen over. Many will stay through the winter until the first sign of spring, and then they flock together and make the return trip north.

Migrating winter waterfowl include tundra swans, snow geese, Canada geese, brants and dabbling and diving ducks. Pied-billed grebes, cormorants, rails and raptors can also be seen during the winter months.

Swans and Geese

Of these winter visitors, the tundra swan travels the farthest. It flies over 4,000 miles to join its kin in Back Bay and Mackay Island. Shallow ponds tend to draw this large white bird. It can be recognized by its long neck, black bill and

Tundra Swan vs

straight neck. The long neck allows it to reach into shallow waters of lakes and ponds and feed on underwater vegetation.

Geese are smaller than swans but larger than ducks. They forage primarily on rootstocks and shoots of grasses and sedges on land and in water.

The snow goose is also a large white bird and can be distinguished from the tundra swan in flight by its black wing tips and pink beak. They often migrate in large flocks at high altitudes to coastal marshlands. Smaller flocks are more frequently observed as they noisily fly back and forth between their winter feeding grounds.

Snow Geese

The Canada goose usually migrates at low altitudes in V-shaped formations. It is recognized by its black head, long black neck, white "chin strap," and white breast. These birds have become quite comfortable in this area and some stay year-round.

Canada Geese
vs

Less common is a smaller and stockier goose, the Atlantic brant, a transient that stays only for the winter. Its field marks are a solid black head and chest. For more information on the Canada goose and the Atlantic brant, see page 16.

Dabblers

Dabbling ducks are surface feeding ducks who forage primarily on plants in shallow waters. Frequently seen with bottom end up, they dip into the water to feed on vegetation growing on the bottom. Dabblers' legs are positioned toward the middle of the body to ease in their feeding techniques. When frightened, they are able to fly directly into the air from the water.

The most common duck of shallow ponds, creeks and marshes is the mallard. They are year-round residents that begin forming pairs in autumn and breeding in early spring.

Mallards

vs

Pintails are fast, high fliers that move south early in the fall. The long, pointed tail feathers distinguish them from other ducks.

Shovelers swim slowly with their heads half submerged in the water. They are identified by their broad, spoon-shaped bills, which they use as a shovel to scoop up food as they move through the water.

Pintails

Wood ducks are the most colorful and elusive of the dabbling ducks. Hollow trees near water are used as a nesting site. Wood duck nesting boxes are often put up as a substitute for hollow trees to attract them to an area.

ps

Wood Duck

Divers

Divers include ducks, grebes and cormorants that swim underwater to forage on roots, seeds, fish or other aquatic animals. They have difficulty walking on land as their legs are positioned to the rear of their bodies. When alarmed, they disappear beneath the surface and reappear either a great distance away or in the reeds where they are hidden. To take flight, diving ducks run along the surface of the water to build up speed before lifting off. Awkward on land, they spend most of their time in water.

Cormorants are dark, slender-bodied birds with a hooked bill that is usually tilted upward when swimming. The bill and throat pouch are yellowish underneath. Lacking oil glands in their wings, they are frequently seen perched over the water with their wings spread outward to dry before taking flight.

Cormorant

The ruddy duck is a stiff-tailed duck that normally swims with its tail feathers held upright.

Mergansers are fish-eating ducks that pursue their prey underwater. They have serrated edges on their bills that help them to catch and hold on to the fish.

Ruddy Duck   *ps*

Other diving ducks include redheads and canvasbacks. Redheads are not usually seen in the numbers they once were due to the loss of

Red-breasted Merganser   *ps*

underwater grasses. Greater and lesser scaup are bay ducks which are occasionally seen in Back Bay and near Mackay Island in the spring and fall.

A ducklike bird that is seen in coastal waters all year is the pied-billed grebe. Swimming low in the water it disappears quickly out of sight when spotted and re-emerges a short time later farther away.

Pied-billed Grebes   vs

Rails, Coots and Gallinules

Rails, coots and gallinules are all marsh inhabitants and members of the same family. Their chattering voices are more often heard at dawn and at dusk.

Rails are secretive birds that live among the grasses or wade between them at the water's edge. When spotted, instead of flying, they simply disappear in the reeds or underbrush without a

King Rail   vs

sound or stirring the grasses. When flight does occur, it is only for a short distance before the rail drops out of sight, its color blending in with the marsh background.

Coots and gallinules are duck-like birds that are more adapted to life in water than on land. The small head which nods up and down as they swim distinguishes them from ducks. Coots prefer open, shallow waters and often gather in large flocks in their southern winter grounds. Gallinules, also called moorhens, are less sociable and prefer being hidden by the grasses in more secluded waters.

American Coot   Common Gallinule   vs

Mackay Island History

Contiguous to Knotts Island is Mackay Island, located in the southwestern portion of a marshy peninsula. To the south is Currituck Sound with Back Bay to the north. Mackay Island's name can be traced to an old colonial land purchase. In 1761 John Mackie purchased "Orphan's Island." Over the years the name was changed to Mackay Island of today.

The land now occupied by the refuge was at one time owned by Joseph Palmer Knapp who founded the organization that would become Ducks Unlimited. After Mr. Knapp's death in 1951, the island was sold and the large estate built by Knapp fell into disrepair. In 1961, the U.S. Fish and Wildlife Service purchased the land to provide habitat for

Photo by Ed Schiller

migratory birds, particularly the greater snow goose. This land is located on the Atlantic Flyway and attracts thousands of migratory birds in winter. This large group of migratories along this part of the Atlantic Flyway pay a winter visit to the waterways surrounding Mackay Island and Knotts Island and connect to the south to Currituck Sound.

The word "Currituck" was derived from the Algonquian Indian word believed to mean "the land of the wild goose." The name "Currituck" has endured no less than 20 different spellings over many years on maps and in legal documents. The current spelling seems to have been adopted in 1765 (Currituck Council Tricentennial Committee, 1970).

Artifacts found on the island are evidence that American Indians once lived here. The early Indians who lived in this part of North Carolina may have used the same divisions of a calendar year as the Tidewater area Indians of Virginia. To both groups, related by language, the five seasons related to food sources. When the growing season ended, the darkening of the sky by thousands of migratory birds signaled not only a new season, but a new food source. The five seasons are listed as: "the Budding of the Corn, the Earing of the Corn, the Highest Sun, the corn gathering, and the Call of the Goose. The winter season was called, Cohonks, after the call of the wild goose, and this was their means of counting years, implying so many annual returns of that fowl" (Whichard, 1959).

Part 3

Back Bay

Back Bay

Back Bay is the largest inland body of water in the City of Virginia Beach. More land in Virginia Beach (33.7%) drains directly into Back Bay than any other watershed (City of Virginia Beach, 1998). The area commonly referred to as Back Bay is actually a collection of smaller bays that include North Bay, Shipps Bay, Redhead Bay and Sand Bay with Back Bay proper to the south of all of these.

Back Bay's name is fitting as it is a bay located in back of a dune line that separates Virgnia's southernmost barrier spit from the ocean. Bordered by maritime forests, the blackwater streams that empty into Back Bay may be the reason that on some very old maps, its name was listed as "Black Bay." Today the blackwater streams still empty tannins into the bay and it is largely a freshwater bay. The waters of the ocean rarely breach the dunes as they have in the past, washing salt water into the bay and there is only a slight saltiness from intrusion of water from Currituck Sound to the south.

While Back Bay is tempting for paddlers with its broad expanses of water, it is not always the most pleasant

Location

Back Bay is located in the southeastern corner of Virginia. To the east is a narrow strip of land that separates Back Bay from the Atlantic Ocean and includes Sandbridge, Back Bay National Wildlife Refuge and False Cape State Park. To the west is the mainland of Virginia Beach and part of Back Bay National Wildlife Refuge.

Access Points

A. Back Bay Landing Road
B. Mill Landing Road
C. Lovitt's Landing
D. Horn Point Canoe & Kayak Launch
E. Lotus Garden
F. Little Island Park
G. Refuge Headquarters
H. Barbour's Hill
I. False Cape Landing
J. Wash Woods

of places to paddle. Strong winds from the northeast can drive a lot of water out of Back Bay leaving some areas high and damp. Winds from any direction can make paddling uncomfortable because this area is so vast. It is recommended that the paddler consult a weather report before planning a trip to Back Bay and carry a GPS, compass, map or chart while on the water. Not to dissuade one from paddling this body of water, Back Bay is a beautiful place to explore.

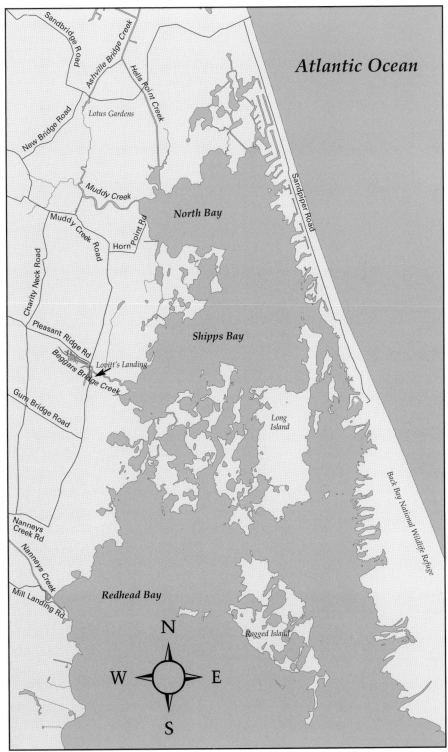

Atlantic Ocean

Sandbridge Road

Ashville Bridge Creek

Hells Point Creek

Lotus Gardens

New Bridge Road

Muddy Creek

North Bay

Muddy Creek Road

Horn Point Rd

Charity Neck Road

Sandpiper Road

Pleasant Ridge Rd

Shipps Bay

Beggars Bridge Creek

Lovitt's Landing

Gum Bridge Road

Long Island

Back Bay National Wildlife Refuge

Nanneys Creek Rd

Nanneys Creek

Mill Landing Rd

Redhead Bay

Ragged Island

N
W E
S

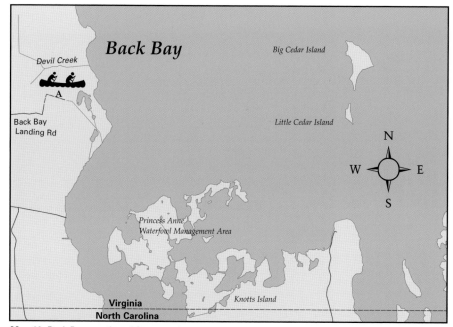

Map 10: Back Bay, continued from previous page © *Vickie Shufer*

Access Points
A. Back Bay Landing Road

Directions: From the oceanfront in Virginia Beach, go south on Pacific Avenue/U.S. 60 and cross the bridge at Rudee Inlet. After crossing the bridge the road name changes to General Booth Boulevard/Route 615. Continue south approximately 4 miles until you reach Princess Anne Road. Look for signs that say Mackay Island NWR, Back Bay NWR. Turn south (left) at the light onto Princess Anne Road and follow it approximately 13 miles to Back Bay Landing Road, then turn east (left). Follow the road to the end, about 1¾ miles, until you come to the parking lot for the Trojan Marsh Tract of the Princess Anne Wildlife Management Area. There is a boat launch and channel that leads to Back Bay.

Barbara White, Alexis Koehling &
Al White launching a boat

vs

Launch site at Mill Landing Road   *vs*

B. Mill Landing Boat Ramp

Directions: From General Booth Boulevard, go south on Princess Anne Road approximately 5½ miles to Mill Landing Road and turn east (left). Go about 3 miles on Mill Landing Road and look for the large parking lot on the west side. This is the Mill Landing Road Boat Ramp, known by locals as Old Game Warden Headquarters Boat Ramp. The warden's headquarters used to be the building on the left at the end of the road. Today it is privately owned. The ramp is also the access point for Nanneys Creek. The boat ramp is across the street from the parking lot.

C. Lovitt's Landing

Directions: Follow Princess Anne Road/Route 615 south toward Pungo. Continue through the intersection at Indian River Road for ⅔ mile and turn east (left) onto Muddy Creek Road. Follow the winding road for about 4¼ miles to the bridge crossing Beggars Bridge Creek. The parking area and boat ramp are south of the bridge on the east side of Muddy Creek Road.

Informal launch site at Beggars Bridge Creek   *vs*

vs

D. Horn Point Canoe and Kayak Launch

Directions: Follow the directions for Lovitt's Landing to Muddy Creek Road. Go east on Muddy Creek Road approximately 2½ miles until you come to Horn Point Road and turn left. Follow the road to the end. This non-motorized boat launch is a joint project between the City of Virginia Beach and the U.S. Fish and Wildlife Service. The site is managed by Back Bay National Wildlife Refuge and consists of several parking spaces, a boardwalk and trail leading paddlers to a canoe/kayak launch site.

North Bay paddler

vs

E. *Lotus Gardens*

Directions: From the intersection of Princess Anne Road and Sandbridge Road, turn east onto Sandbridge Road and follow the signs to Sandbridge. After about 2 miles the road makes a sharp turn to the east. Another ¼ mile, just after the intersection of Sandbridge Road and New Bridge Road, you will see the Lotus Gardens on the right. The put-in point is just east of New Bridge Road. Park to be safe from traffic on Sandbridge Road.

The City of Virginia Beach Department of Parks and Recreation maintains the Lotus Garden Park on Sandbridge Road, the current launch site for this water trail. The park is open year-round, dawn to dusk. There are picnic tables, but currently no restroom facilities and no drinking water.

To get to Blue Pete's Restaurant on Muddy Creek Road (a possible take-out point or launch site, either with permission only), turn south on New Bridge Road and after 1³⁄₁₀ miles, New Bridge will intersect with Indian River Road. Turn southeast (left) and in ½ mile Indian River intersects with North Muddy Creek Road. Turn east (left) on North Muddy Creek Road and travel ⁶⁄₁₀ of a mile along the road that curves through farmland and cypress swamp. Look for the sign for **Blue Pete's Seafood and Steak Restaurant** on the north (left) side of the road at 1400 North Muddy Creek Road. For hours of operation, call 757-426-2005. For more information visit www.bluepetes.com.

F. Little Island

Directions: From General Booth Boulevard/Route 615 (see directions for Access Point A), turn south (left) at the light onto Princess Anne Road/Route 615. Follow the signs for Sandbridge Road/Route 629 to the Sandbridge community, about 3¼ miles, and turn south (right) on Sandpiper Road. Go almost 4 miles to Little Island Park on the east side (left).

Little Island Park is operated by the City of Virginia Beach Department of Parks and Recreation and has 200 parking spaces. Access for canoes and kayaks is on the west side of Sandpiper Road across from the park. This access is a sandy beach marked by a sign. From this point one may paddle south to Back Bay's Visitor Contact Station, other points south, or to any location on the east side of the Bay (or the west side if one is ambitious).

Robert Frisch launching his kayak at Little Island   *vs*

Wind Tides

As with all of Back Bay and its tributaries, water levels can change drastically in a day's time (or less). Southerly winds bring water up from Currituck Sound, resulting in high water, while northerly winds push the water out.

G. Refuge Headquarters

Directions: Follow the directions to Little Island Park but continue past the park a short distance. The road makes a sharp turn to the east and another turn to the south to the entrance gate of Back Bay National Wildlife Refuge. There is an entrance fee unless you have a Duck Stamp (available from the refuge). Follow this road about a mile to the parking lot at the Back Bay National Wildlife Refuge Visitor Contact Station (pictured above), There is a sandy beach from which a canoe or kayak can easily be launched.

Scott Ziemer, Chris, Isaac and Sam Kirkey at Back Bay NWR launch site   *vs*

Paddling Sections

1. **(A) Back Bay Landing Road to Devil Creek, 6 miles, round-trip**
2. **(B) Nanneys Creek to Nanneys Creek Road, 2½ miles, one-way**
3. **(C) Lovitt's Landing to Shipps Bay, ½ mile**
4. **(D) Horn Point Road to Muddy Creek, 5 miles round-trip**
5. **(E) Lotus Gardens to North Bay, 5½ miles**
6. **(F) Little Island Park to (G) Refuge Headquarters, 1¾ miles**
7. **(G) Refuge Headquarters to (H) Barbour's Hill, about 4½ miles**
8. **(H) Barbour's Hill to (I) False Cape Landing, 2½ miles**
9. **(I) False Cape Landing to (J) Wash Woods, 1½ miles**

Section 1. (A) Back Bay Landing Road to Devil Creek, about 6 miles, round-trip

The canal leading from the boat ramp to Back Bay is ⁷⁄₁₀ mile and is mostly straight, characteristic of dredged waterways. Spoil banks on either side are characteristic of disturbed areas, with loblolly pines, black cherries and red maples forming a wall of shrubery on both sides of the waterway. They are just large enough to provide a minimum amount of shade on a hot, summer day.

Once you have reached the bay, go left and look to the northeast. The large buildings you see on the other side of the bay are the condos at Sandbridge, near Little Island Park. Continue paddling along the western shoreline. Phragmites, big cordgrass and black needlerush are the dominant plants bordering Back Bay.

After going around the first point, you will be heading north. On the

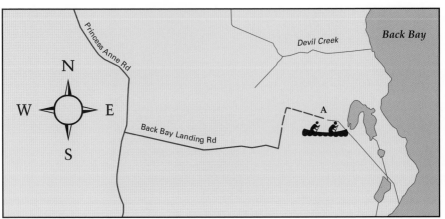

Map 11: Back Bay Landing Road to Devil Creek

62

© Vickie Shufer

Seashore Mallow

Marsh plants along Devil Creek   *vs*

west side of the bay are markers from the game department. Look for marker #3, which will be just before the opening leading west. This is the entrance to Devil Creek, a little over 1 mile from the canal. The islands immediately east of the opening are Big Cedar Island and Little Cedar Island, both under the management of False Cape State Park. Once you have entered Devil Creek, the diversity of plant life increases. Rose mallow, seashore mallow, swamp milkweed, saltmarsh loosestrife, water parsnip and sawgrass are some of the plants growing along the shoreline.

Continue paddling west about 1 mile, until the creek forks. The right fork will take you deeper into the marsh with some woody growth that provides cover for larger animals. The tracks they leave behind can be seen on sandy beaches along the waterway. Bobcat, otter, raccoon and nutria are among the animals whose tracks have been observed here.

Bobcat Track

Vickie studies tracks in the sand
at the edge of Devil Creek   63   *lg*

vs

Princess Anne Wildlfe Management Area

The Princess Anne Wildlife Management Area, totaling 1,546 acres, is comprised of three tracts: the Trojan Marsh, the Whitehurst tract and the Pocahontas Marsh. Only the Trojan Marsh, located at the end of Back Bay Landing Road, has boat access. This is also the headquarters for the Management Area. The Whitehurst tract is north of the Trojan Marsh and can be accessed by vehicle. The Trojan Marsh and the Whitehurst tract are both described in the "Virginia Birding and Wildlife Trail."

Man-made impoundments were dug as a part of the game department's management plan. Water levels are controlled to promote plant growth for wintering and migrating waterfowl.

Keep in mind that as a wildlife management area, it is a hunting area, especially in the fall and winter months. Check with the Virginia Department of Game and Inland Fisheries for the current dates and regulations at www.dgif.virginia.gov.

Canal leading from Back Bay Landing Road to Back Bay   *vs*

Section 2. (B) Nanneys Creek to Nanneys Creek Road, 2½ miles one-way

To get to Nanneys Creek, paddle west from the boat ramp. Soon after launching there is a fork in the creek. This is an oxbow and is very shallow at low water. It is best to continue straight unless the water is high.

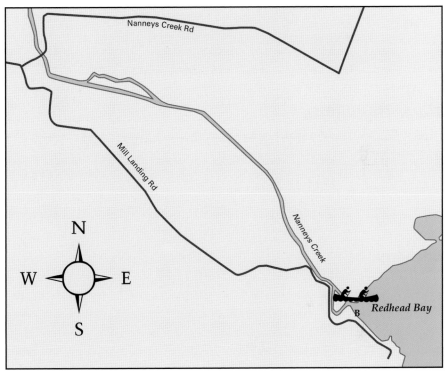

Map 12: Nanneys Creek   © *Vickie Shufer*

Nawney Creek or Nanneys Creek?

Talk to the locals and ask about the name of the creek. Most will say the creek is "Nanneys," or "Nanney" – not "Nawneys." The current road name on maps is Nanneys Creek Road while the creek is written as Nawney Creek. Apparently at some point in time, a sign-maker or map maker made an error and "Nawney" became the published name. We are told that the locals hope the old name will be restored on signage and future maps. As early as 1691, this little creek was known as "Nani" or "Nanni Creek." In notes of a meeting at the club house on the third of June, 1691, it was one of the dividing points in Princess Anne County tithable areas, "Evan Jones Nani Creek to Matchapungo and so southerly..." (Minute Book, Vol. 1. 1601-1714, page 21).

High water line on bald cypress trees on Nanneys Creek   *vs*

River Highlights

Most of the surrounding area is a freshwater marsh, with a border of bald cypress trees and their knees forming a bulkhead at the water's edge. The water line on the trees indicates recent water levels. Black needlerush, big cordgrass and cattails dominate the marsh with rose mallow and waxmyrtle mixed in with them. Look for great blue herons, kingfishers, woodpeckers and migratory songbirds. Soaring above may be turkey vultures, hawks or eagles.

Bayberry

A common coastal shrub that is found throughout the Back Bay area is bayberry, also called waxmyrtle. This plant was used historically by the Indians and later the settlers. The grayish colored berries have a waxy coating that is extracted by boiling, cooling and purifying. The wax is fragrant, greenish, and brittle. It is used for making beautiful fragrant candles, soap and other products (Erichsen-Brown, 1979).

Bayberries   *vs*

A Kettle Soaring

Often while we are on group walks or
kayak and canoe eco-tours, someone will
say, "Look, eagles!" We all look immediately
upward to see, more times than not, the turkey vultures.
Granted, it has almost the wing span of an eagle, soaring with a 6 foot spread
versus the 8 foot span of the bald eagle, and while it is not our national symbol,
it is still a magnificent study in flight. This large bird with a small head is
often called turkey buzzard, probably so-named for the red featherless head
which resembles the head of the wild turkey. It is the adult bird who has a red
head and ivory beak while juveniles have a dark grey head and beak.

Most people associate vultures with unsavoriness, due to their highly
"specialized" eating habits. But, this large bird does a remarkable job of cleaning
up the environment of non-living animals. The turkey vulture can locate
carrion not only by sight, but also by its exceptional sense of smell. To be
scientific, it is the decay gas mercaptan they can detect up to parts per trillion
(Needham, 2006). Their acute sense of smell comes in very handy in detecting
decaying animals as a food source, as they have weak beaks which deter them
from killing prey. They have been known to eat vegetative matter and young
or weak animals if their preferred foods are unavailable. Their selective eating
habits require them to sometimes wait several days for their "dinner" to get
soft enough for consumption; they never eat animals in advanced decay.
These large scavengers prefer an herbivore to a carnivore because "it is much
tastier" (Needham, 2006). How the turkey vulture can digest its favorite
foods is another interesting fact: their stomachs exude digestive acids that kill
the harmful microorganisms and bacteria that would sicken almost any other
animal.

Back to their soaring habits, the turkey vulture uses updrafts to gain
altitude in looking for food. Raptor expert, Reese Lukei reports, "The most
identifiable flight characteristic of the TV is the 'V' shape or strong dihedral
of the wings, the two-toned black and grey color of the under side of the
wings, and the way it rocks back and forth without flapping its wings as it
rides a thermal." Their circling is not necessarily an indicator of the location
of a dead animal, as most of us dread to think. A group of vultures is known
as a "kettle." Seeing them in the sky circling and circling, rising ever higher
on air columns, one can imagine steam rising from a hot, whistling kettle.
This kitchen simile is an easy way to remember the vultures' "group" name
and makes for an interesting way to introduce the unusual *Cathartes aura* to a
group of onlookers. Their scientific name comes from the Greek *katharsis*
referring no doubt to the cleansing of the land by this scavenger, with *aura*

meaning breeze. Never mind the turkey vultures' supposed reputation. A soaring kettle taking to the breezes of the updrafts is indeed a wonder of nature.

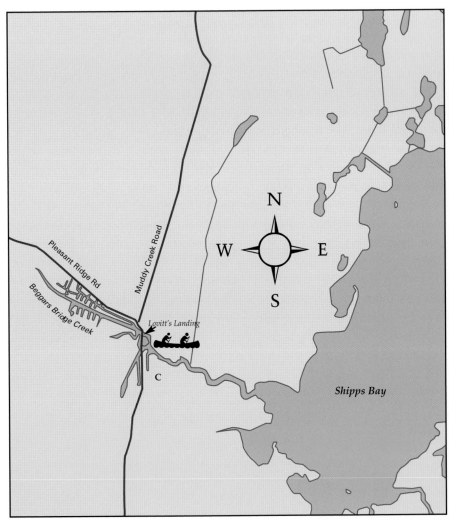

Map 13: Beggars Bridge Creek   © Vickie Shufer

Section 3. (C) Lovitt's Landing to Shipps Bay, ½ mile, one-way

From Lovitt's Landing, the paddler has the option of going west on Beggars Bridge Creek toward the headwaters, or paddling east to Shipps Bay which connects with Back Bay. It's about ½ mile either way. Going west, the waterway is more narrow and protected from the winds. After crossing under the bridge, the marshes give way to a forested swamp with bald cypress, swamp black gums, red maples and other hardwoods bordering the creek. Waxmyrtles, groundsel bushes and swamp roses are among the understory plants, both providing a source of food for songbirds that spend their winters in the Back Bay area. An abundance of wood duck boxes are an indication that wood ducks frequent the quiet headwaters. Great blue herons and kingfishers are commonly seen on the creek.

Groundsel Bush   vs

Paddling east from Beggars Bridge, the creek widens and is mostly marshland with phragmites, cattails and big cordgrass along the borders. About ¼ mile east of the bridge, look for an opening on the north side immediately past the rip-rap bulkhead. The narrow waterway offers protection from the wind as well as a greater diversity of flora and fauna. Follow this waterway for almost 1 mile, until you come to an old, dilapidated wooden bridge. Evidence of fox, raccoon and opossum can be seen on the bridge. Thickets of young red maples, sweetgums and vines have developed on both sides of the bridge.

Wood Ducks

Wood ducks are one of the most colorful. Iridescent greens, purples and blues are distinctive features of the male wood duck. The grayish-colored female is less bold, blending in with the dark colors of the swamp where she nests and raises her young. Wood ducks are one of the few ducks that nest in southeastern Virginia. They build their nests in cavities or holes in trees where there is shelter, such as dark swamps or tree-bordered rivers. Young ducklings leave the nest soon after hatching by jumping to the ground or water.

Wood Duck Food

Plant foods make up a large part of the wood duck's diet and include submerged aquatic plants such as coontail and pondweed. Duckweed and waterlily are floating-leaves plants that are also a part of their diet. Other foods include the fruits and seeds of arrow arum, black gum, smartweed, wild rice and rice cutgrass.

Back Bay Memories

Back in the mid 1920s my brothers, who were older than I was, loved to go fishing. We lived close to Back Bay and the creek that flowed from Beggars Bridge on Muddy Creek Road out to the Bay. When farm work and studies were slack, they would go out in the yard and start to dig worms. They had no artificial lures for bait then--just long wiggly earthworms.

We had a yellow dog named Fritz who loved to go fishing as much as they did. When he saw them digging worms, he would run and jump on the front seat of our Model-T Ford and wait for them.

Sometimes the boys would let me go along with them. It seemed to me that it was so nice of them to do that. We would go down to Beggars Bridge, get into the boat that was kept there and ride out the creek to the Bay. Then we would go over to the shore and pull up close to the reeds on the edge of the Bay.

It was then that I found out why they were so nice to let me go. They had an ulterior motive. You see, they didn't have an anchor. They would pull some reeds over the back seat of the boat and tell me to sit on them to keep the boat from moving. In other words, I was the anchor.

They came home with fish. I came home with a bad sunburn. But it was fun and I would do it again if I had the chance.

Emily Murden Capps

Lovitt's Landing,
mid 1980s

*Photo Courtesy of
Judy Roehling*

Paddling Tip

To explore the many coves and marsh area of Back Bay, paddlers and other boaters are encouraged to take along a GPS, map or chart. Don't forget to leave a float plan with someone at the home base that includes your time of departure as well as expected time of return.

Section 4. (D) Horn Point Road to Muddy Creek Road, about 5 miles round-trip

From the launch site at Horn Point Road, paddle north about ½ mile until you see the opening to Muddy Creek heading west. Phragmites lines the water's edge on the south side; on the north point is a small, wooded area that serves as a perching area for large birds of prey, including hawks, osprey and maybe even an eagle.

Follow Muddy Creek for about 1½ miles until you come to the fork in the creek. Just before this fork a canal to Blue Pete's Restaurant emerges to the south (left). Paddle west to stay on Muddy Creek. Ashville Bridge Creek is to the north (described on p. 73).

The mostly shaded route from the confluence of Ashville Bridge Creek and Muddy Creek provides welcome relief on a warm summer day. What was marsh now becomes swamp with bald cypress and loblolly pines bordering the creek and a mixed hardwood forest on higher ground. An array of cypress trees in the water can function as a slalom course to test one's steering ability. Two such groups of these trees are within a tenth of a mile from each other.

Exploring the two tributaries that lead north is rewarding on a high water day. At lower water levels, underwater snags and fallen logs prevent a longer trip. Each of these waterways is an old canal gone wild, where the only

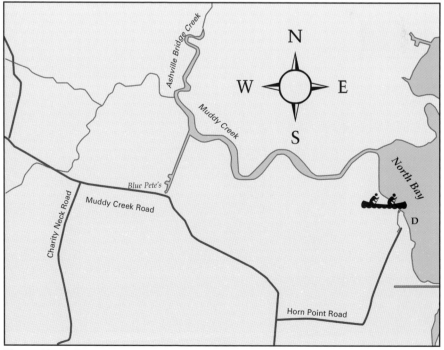

Map 14: Muddy Creek

© Vickie Shufer

sounds are the chorus of frogs, the birds chirping and singing, and an occasional fish jumping out of the water. Along the banks are discarded clam shells that are possibly the remains of an otter or raccoon's dinner. Fallen logs block the paddler from going too far, but nevertheless, these tributaries add some variety to the trip.

Back on the main Muddy Creek route, the western terminus is Muddy Creek Road of which

Discarded clam shells   *vs*

the paddler is fully aware as one gets close to this two lane road. The creek does continue a bit farther on the other side of the road, finally becoming part of a farmland's canal. To keep going on the waterway is tempting, but the road portage would be dangerous as this asphalt section is on a curve.

Reversing the route, paddle back on this creek and look for great blue herons, eastern kingbirds, kingfishers and red-winged blackbirds. These birds along with a variety of dragonflies help keep the insect pests at a minimum.

Cypress and swamp black gum trees provide a slalom course along part of Muddy Creek   *vs*

Section 5. (E) Lotus Garden to North Bay, 5½ miles

Distinctive for being the only water loop trail in the city of Virginia Beach, Virginia, North Bay Loop includes three small creeks: Ashville Bridge Creek, Hells Point Creek and Muddy Creek and offers a unique look at several ecotones.

This circuit paddling trail is easy to reach by road and is an interesting day trip near Sandbridge. The terrain varies from blackwater swamp to forest to open water, and with the exception of Hells Point Creek, most of it is relatively shallow. The easiest paddling route is clockwise around the loop because of predominant northerly winds.

To get to Ashville Bridge Creek, the paddler must immediately portage and launch on the north side of Sandbridge Road or paddle through the culverts that connect the two sides of the creek. The paddler will encounter a few houses, but these in no way detract from the natural scenery. This narrow waterway is treed with bald cypress, loblolly pine and red maple on the east

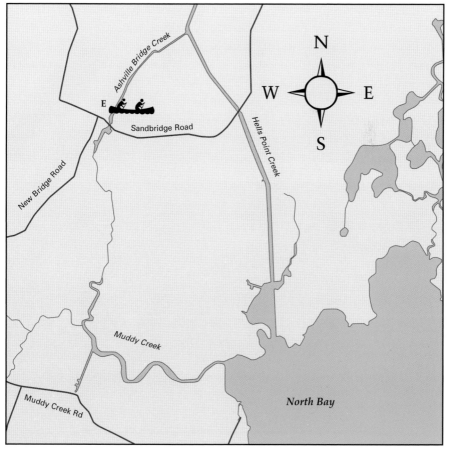

Map 15: Ashville Bridge Creek to North Bay

© Vickie Shufer

73

bank. On the west side is a cattail marsh with arrow arum, rose mallow and waxmyrtle.

After about ½ mile, the paddler will emerge into Hells Point Creek. This is a manmade canal that runs alongside Hells Point Golf Course to the north and west. Turn south (right) to go to the Hells Point Creek. Hells Point Creek is wider than Ashville Bridge Creek and more exposed to the sun. It is a long straight canal with red maple and wild black cherry dominating the banks.

Continuing south past the Hells Point Creek Bridge, the paddler will pass Indian Cove Resort on the west before coming to a patch of woods. Off in the distance to the east is a large nest, possibly belonging to an osprey. There is at least one eagle's nest in Back Bay so keep a sharp eye out for these large birds circling above the bay. This is a good spot to watch for birds of prey, including hawks, osprey and eagles. Binoculars in a watertight container are a blessing.

The creek ends at North Bay, the northernmost bay of the Back Bay collection. Much of the land surrounding this area is part of the more than 8,000 acres that comprise Back Bay National Wildlife Refuge.

If deciding to venture into Back Bay from North Bay, it is best to have a map or chart. To continue on the popular route into Muddy Creek, turn west and paddle along the shoreline. The first creek is Muddy Creek. Here you will enter into a phragmites marsh, with a dense growth of tall reeds on both sides of the creek. Redwing blackbirds and kingbirds are a common sight in these marshes. Look for the hanging nest of the redwing blackbird woven into the grasses.

Paddlers on Ashville Bridge Creek

VS

Continue west on Muddy Creek for about 1½ miles. After making several turns you will come to a fork in the creek. Follow the larger body of water to the north. With a northwest wind this can be shallow going, but persevere; this trip is almost at an end. In about a quarter mile, Ashville Bridge Creek becomes a very narrow band of water. The Lotus Garden Pond will materialize in about three-quarters of a mile. This was the original put-in spot and is now your take-out.

River Highlights

As you paddle west and north, notice the increased diversity of plant life. Black needlerush, big cordgrass, rose mallows, swamp milkweed, and knotweed are among the marsh plants growing here. Several patches of wild rice have made their way into the creek, plus the lotus pads have returned.

Swamp Milkweed

Swamp milkweed is the butterfly weed of the marshes – it is both a host plant and a nectar plant for numerous butterflies. Monarchs are known for laying their eggs on the leaves of milkweed during the summer months. When the eggs hatch, the caterpillars feed on the leaves of the milkweed plant. Later in the summer when the clusters of pink flowers develop, a lot of butterflies, including several types of swallowtails, visit the milkweed for their nectar.

Swamp Milkweed with Swallowtails sipping nectar *vs*

Willow – The 2,400 Year Old Wonder Drug

Native willow trees grow lushly along the banks of Back Bay, helping to hold them in place and prevent erosion. Few paddlers realize that their leaves and bark are rich in a substance called salicin, which is the same chemical that the Greek physician Hippocrates (who lived between 460 B.C. and 377 B.C) prescribed as a fever breaker and pain reliever. Willow was reported by early writers to have been used by American Indians as a drug and for fiber (Erichsen-Brown, 1979). Meadow Sweet (*Spiraea ulmaria*), another plant containing salicin, was also favored by early chemists.

In 1588 Thomas Harriot reported about his excursion from what is now North Carolina north into Virginia. He was accompanied by John White who documented the trip with drawings while Harriot took notes. The writings about willow explain the English use of the plant which apparently was not medicinal: "Willowes good for the making of weares and weeles (traps) to take fishe after the English manner, although the inhabitants use only reedes, which because they are so strong as also flexible, do serve for that turne very well and sufficiently" (Quinn, 1995).

Today's aspirin contains acetylsalicylic acid, first extracted in the 1820s and 1830s from natural ingredients. These breakthrough experiments led to acetyl chloride being added to buffer both the taste and the effect on the stomach. By 1899 the Bayer company in Germany produced aspirin in powder form for doctors to prescribe to patients. Chemists at

Black Willow tree

vs

Bayer gave their "wonder drug" the name Aspirin: the "A" from acetyl chloride, the "spir" from *Spiraea ulmaria* and the "in" merely because it was a common ending name for medicines at the time. In 1915, the first Aspirin was made in tablet form. On an interesting historical note, Aspirin ® was once a trademark owned by Bayer. As a conditional part of the Treaty of Versailles in 1919 after Germany lost World War I, the Bayer company was forced to give up its trademarks: thus, "aspirin" is now written with a lower case "a". Today the world consumes about 40 billion tablets of aspirin a year (inventors.about. com/library/inventors/blaspirin.htm).

The next time you find yourself up a creek without your aspirin and feel a headache coming on, look for a willow tree twig to chew on and remember to say, "Thanks!"

vs

Suggested Sunset Paddle and Dinner Plan

We recommend a unique idea for hungry paddlers. Try part of the North Bay Loop as a sunset trip. Having led kayak tours into this area since the 1980s and using **Blue Pete's Seafood and Steak Restaurant** as the dinner stop, our paddlers have enjoyed this as a relaxing end of day experience.

To paddle to Blue Pete's Restaurant, look for a canal to the south from Muddy Creek (see p. 73). With prior planning and permission this makes an interesting dinner stop and take-out. This is a fine restaurant so be mindful of any dress code and call ahead for reservations.

Blue Pete's was founded in 1973 by Pat Ricks, a former Virginia Beach teacher, who owned the restaurant until 2003. The new owners, K. C. Knauer and her family, operate the restaurant with the same down-home coziness as the former owner. The floor plan with tables arranged to take in the views offered by the huge water-facing windows, offers exceptional glimpses of the changing colors of the evening. The 250-seat restaurant is named for a ducklike bird once found in very large numbers on the nearby Back Bay.

Do take the time to plan this trip by running a shuttle vehicle to Blue Pete's before beginning the paddle trip. Then paddlers will not have to paddle back to the launch site in the dark. Sunsets over the water with colors reflecting, birds flying in for the evening, and the fishermen long gone all make for a quiet and interesting paddling trip. If a short trip is desired, put in at the Lotus Pond and paddle basically south. Look to the south (right) to find the opening to the canal that ends at Blue Pete's. If paddling from Horn Point, the canal on Muddy Creek will be on your left. When approaching the restaurant, be observant for the wading birds that feed in the canal.

Great Blue Heron at edge of canal   *vs*

Photo by Paul Shufer

Who is Blue Pete?

Blue pete is another name for the American coot, a ducklike diving bird that is sometimes seen traveling in rafts on open waters. The small head which nods up and down as it swims helps to identify it. Coots are more adapted to life in water than on land and must first run across the water before becoming airborne.

Wild Rice

Wild rice is a native grass that has historically been a food source for American Indians and wildlife. The species growing in the Back Bay area is the same species that is grown and harvested in northern states as gourmet food item. Today the wild rice growing in the Back Bay area is mainly a food source for wildlife. As the grains mature, red-wing blackbirds flock to the rice fields. Wading birds eat the seeds that fall into the water while diving ducks feed on grains that settle to the bottom. Blue-wing teals, black ducks, mallards, wood ducks and Canada geese arrive after the seeds have matured but will dig into the soil to feed on the rhizomes.

Wild rice grows best in shallow lakes, tidal fresh-water streams, ponds or marshes with soft mud bottoms and water six inches to three feet deep (Hugo, 1987). Mature grains that have fallen into the water will germinate in the spring if conditions are right.

Wild rice is easy to identify. The female flowers where the seeds develop are at the top of the stalk. The male bell-shaped flowers are beneath the female, assuring that cross-pollination will take place.

Vickie harvesting wild rice

lg

Grace Sherwood

One of the most famous residents of this area was Grace Sherwood, also known as "The Witch of Pungo." Grace was accused of witchcraft in 1706 by several of her neighbors and was brought to trial at the courthouse then located near the Lynnhaven River in the northern part of the jurisdictional area known as Princess Anne County. Grace agreed to a trial by water. She was found guilty on July 10, 1706 after being ducked in the Lynnhaven River and floating rather than sinking (which would have proved her innocence). It is interesting to note that on this same day, the court records show orders for a new "Ducking Stool" and "a new pair of Stocks and Pillory ye old being rotten" (Minute Book, 1706). She was given a seven-year sentence and reacquired 145 acres of land in 16 June 1714 in exchange for "2 lbs. Tobacco, &c."(Nugent, 1992). Grace was the only woman in Princess Anne County to be granted land by the capital at Williamsburg during 1714. The land was part of the property that her father, John White, had given to Grace and her husband, James Sherwood, when they married. It is known that Grace had to pay court costs and perhaps her land was kept from her while she was imprisoned. During her imprisonment her three sons were cared for by some of the White family who lived on Knotts Island. Some of these descendants of Grace's family still live in this North Carolina community.

Art Courtesy of
William Rylance

Grace's Legacy

Grace's farmland was at Muddy Creek bordered by a pocosin and the creek now called Ashville Bridge Creek. Muddy Creek and Muddy Creek Road retain their 18th century names, as do some locations on the Western side of the Lynnhaven River, the site of her ducking. Named because of our famous Grace Sherwood, Witch Duck Point, Witch Duck Bay and Witch Duck Road recall the legacy of the woman who proclaimed to all that she was not a witch, but a healer well-versed in the use of herbs. She died in 1740 at age 80 and is still the subject of local folklore as "The Witch of Pungo," made famous in a book of the same name by late beloved local author, Louisa Venable Kyle.

Saving Grace

Through the tireless efforts of local historian Belinda Nash, Grace was exonerated by the 70th governor of Virginia, Timothy Kaine at exactly 10 a.m. on the 300th anniversary of the trial by water. It was on July 10, 2006 that a crowd assembled once again near the banks of the Lynnhaven River to be a part of Grace's history. The mayor of Virginia Beach, Meyera Oberndorf read the proclamation that restored Grace's good name from the stigma of being accused of witchcraft. News of this historic event was recorded in newspapers in England and Scotland, as well as many papers in the Unites States including the *Wall Street Journal*. Several magazines as diverse as *Time* and *Ladies Home Journal* reported on saving Grace. In Grace's own words supposedly recorded 300 years ago, "I be not a witch!" is now a legal statement of truth.

Statue of Grace Sherwood on
Witchduck Road

Photo by Deni Norred

History of the Lotus Garden

The present **Lotus Garden Pond** was originally the site of a massive growth of American lotus plants. During the 1950's the Cape Henry Woman's Club celebrated the rare plant by hosting the Lotus Festival. Over the years, the lotus plants gradually disappeared and the festival was discontinued. However the memory of the plants continued to be sustained by a luncheon held annually at the Tabernacle United Methodist Church, located within a short walking distance from the pond. The pond's park site was established by the Cape Henry Woman's Club in 1975.

The exact cause of the demise of the lotus plants was never determined. But in 2004, while paddling the creek, two or three lotus pads were spotted. Hopeful that this might mark their return, we watched for them in the coming year and were rewarded to find several large patches of the beautiful flower. Today they are thriving once again.

Lotus plants are easy to identify by their large, umbrella-like leaves sitting on green stalks and yellow blossoms which rise several inches above the water. The plant is a native to Virginia Beach.

Please do not destroy or pick these beautiful flowers or any part of them. Try to avoid paddling through what are now large concentrations of plants at the Lotus Garden Pond, very visible in late summer and early fall.

Section 5. (F) Little Island Park to (G) Refuge Headquarters, 1¾ miles

From the launch site at Little Island, paddling south, the larger island immediately seen is Long Island and a part of the refuge. Stay to the east of the island to go the refuge headquarters. You will pass a couple of osprey nests along the way and numerous wading birds. After you've passed the second smaller island, look for the cove to the east. The Visitor Contact Station and parking lot are visible from the water.

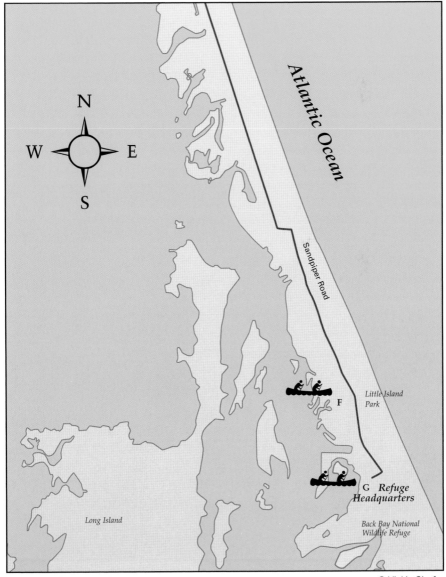

Map 16: Little Island Park to Refuge Headquarters

© Vickie Shufer

Little Island Park

Little Island Park consists of 144 acres and is open from 5:30 a.m. until sundown. Fees from Memorial Day Weekend through Labor Day Weekend apply. Call the park for information at 757-426-0013. To reserve a park shelter, call 757-385-2550.

From Memorial Day through Labor Day Weekend lifeguards are on duty from 9:30 A.M. to 6 P.M. The park has restrooms, several vending machines, lighted tennis courts, basketball courts and shelters for picnics. The 775-foot beach north of the fishing pier is designated for surfing and the 2000-foot beach to the south of the pier is designated for swimming and fishing. Kayaks can be launched from the surfing beach beyond the tennis courts. The fishing pier is open April through October with a fee per day. The fising pier, while open year-round, has limited operating hours November 1 - March 31. For those who plan to camp overnight at False Cape State Park, it is permissible to leave your car in the parking lot, but do notify a park attendant at the Little Island Park office, located in the old Coast Guard station or leave a sign on the dashboard of your car that says "False Cape Guest."

Little Island Park before the neighboring
condos were built

Photo courtesy of
Virginia Beach Dept. of Parks & Recreation

A Haunting at Little Island Station?

Located 14 miles from the Cape Henry Lighthouse stands the last large building of Little Island Station. Formerly the U.S. Life-Saving Station Number 4, originally completed in 1878 and later the Little Island Coast Guard Station, its first keeper was Abel Belanga, appointed January 3, 1879. Ask a particular employee of the Virginia Beach Department of Parks and Recreation (that now manages the property) and he will tell you that the old building is haunted! It is believed that this has happened as a result of one of the East Coast's most tragic shipwrecks.

On the cold stormy day of January 8, 1887 the German ship *Elisabeth* ran aground in a snowstorm at what is now Sandbridge. A rescue party of Captain Belanga, his brother James, his brother-in-law and five surfmen attempted to rescue the 22 man crew in the extremely rough water. All but two of the 29 men died as a result of the attempted rescue. This tragedy was a horrible event in old Princess Anne County and disastrous to the local Life-Saving Services. A descendant of the Captain, Marshall Belanga who lives near Sandbridge, maintains that the shipwreck still lies about 200 yards off the beach.

The former Coast Guard Station that is now in use as park property was built in 1925 and the former station building that was used by Captain Belanga and his surfmen was destroyed in the August 1933 hurricane that hammered the Virginia and Carolina coast. Even though the keeper and his men could never have set foot in the newer station building, it is nevertheless thought that brave Captain Abel Belanga's benevolent spirit is there. The current building was added to the Virginia Beach Historical Register on March 15, 2001.

Little Island Coast Guard Station

Section 6. (G) Refuge Headquarters to (H) Barbour's Hill – 4½ miles

Depending on wind conditions, this can be a fairly easy paddle. However, if the wind picks up or a storm suddenly develops, it can very quickly become difficult. Check the weather forecast before venturing out.

Numerous coves on the eastern side of the bay allow for many bird-watching opportunities. Look for great blue and little blue herons, green-backed herons, tri-colored herons, great egrets, snowy egrets, glossy ibis, yellowlegs, northern harrier, osprey and numerous other marsh birds as you paddle this stretch.

Paddling Tip

When observing high-flying birds, the paddler, looking upwards, sometimes experiences a quick turnover of his/her craft. By placing a hand forward on the cockpit combing before looking up is an easy way to keep one's balance and stay dry.

Back Bay National Wildlife Refuge

Back Bay National Wildlife Refuge contains over 8,000 acres of beach, dunes, woodland, farm fields and marshes. The majority of the marshlands are on islands located within the waters of Back Bay. The refuge provides habitat for migratory snow geese, tundra swans, a large variety of ducks and a wide assortment of other wildlife, including several threatened and endangered species.

The Visitor Contact Station is located a little over a mile from the southern end of Sandpiper Road. An outdoor kiosk describes the immediate area and the types of seasonal wildlife that may be seen. Hiking trails lead through the marshes as well as over the dunes to the beach. A new addition to this site is a boardwalk birding trail that is part of the Charles Kuralt Trail. An overlook at the end of the trail gives a glimpse into the surrounding marsh environment.

The Visitor Contact Station hours are 8:00 a.m. – 4:00 p.m. weekdays, 9:00 a.m. – 4:00 p.m. weekends. The Visitor Contact Station is closed Saturdays, December through March and on holidays with the exception of Memorial Day, July 4 and Labor Day. Dike roads are closed from November 1 to April 1. Outdoor facilities are open daily dawn to dusk.

For more information, call Back Bay National Wildlife Refuge at 757-721-2412 or visit www.fws.gov/backbay.

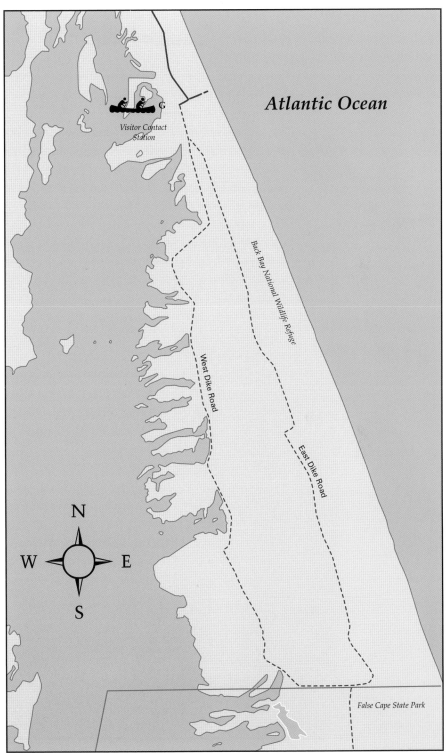

Atlantic Ocean

Visitor Contact Station

G

Back Bay National Wildlife Refuge

West Dike Road

East Dike Road

N
W   E
S

False Cape State Park

Map 17: Back Bay National Wildlife Refuge
to False Cape State Park

© *Vickie Shufer*

Wading Birds

Wading birds along the east coast include herons, egrets, glossy and

Glossy Ibis

occasionally white ibis, yellowlegs and several types of sandpipers. Herons and egrets are closely related birds with long, slender necks that they tuck back on their shoulders while in flight. They nest in large colonies, usually in trees, near the water. Ibis are sometimes seen with the herons and egrets and can be distinguished from them by their long, down curved beak. The neck remains extended while in flight.

Great Egret

Historically wading birds were abundant along the coastal plain. However, the courtship plumage of the males nearly brought them to extinction in the late 19th and early 20th centuries. The plumes were highly sought after by millineries for hat decorations. The Migratory Bird Treaty Act in 1918 brought this enterprise to a halt (Virginia Department of Game & Inland Fisheries, 1989).

Green-backed Heron

Wading birds are once again common in these areas where they are able to nest and raise their young. Loss of habitat is now their biggest threat. The remote islands in Back Bay and Currituck Sound provide them with the nesting sites they need.

Most of the wading birds go south for the winter. Great blue herons and great egrets can be seen all year, although there is a shift in the population. Herons that are here in the winter months go north in the spring, while those who were farther south come here to nest.

Little Blue Heron

Great Blue Heron

Snowy Egret   *Photos by Paul Shufer*

Section 7. (H) Barbour's Hill to (I) False Cape Landing, 2½ miles

From the boat dock at Barbour's Hill, looking immediately west, is Ragged Island. Just to the south of Ragged Island is Big Cedar Island, followed by Little Cedar Island. With marshes along the edges and a maritime forest that includes live oaks and loblolly pines, these islands are home to a large number of herons, egrets, osprey and other marsh birds. Ragged Island is a part of Back Bay National Wildlife Refuge while Big and Little Cedar Islands are a part of False Cape State Park.

Soon after leaving the dock at Barbour's Hill is a small inlet going east known as South Inlet. Take the time to explore this inlet. The narrow waterway is usually calm, even on a windy day, and allows an opportunity to observe great blue herons, great egrets, wood ducks, turtles, occasionally otters, and other wildlife. Red-tail hawks, osprey and bald eagles can sometimes be seen flying overhead.

Just past South Inlet is a larger cove known as Spratts Cove. Phragmites dominates this marsh. Cattails, big cordgrass and black needlerush provide cover and nesting habitat for rails, woodcocks and red-wing blackbirds.

After passing Spratts Cove is an even larger cove. About halfway around the cove is False Cape Landing. Boat docks are available for tying up a canoe or kayak. A sandy bottom allows for easy access to put-in or take-out. There is also a campground at this site. Keep in mind there is no drinking water here. An old boat house used to stand here, but after being battered by a number of nor'easters and hurricane force winds, it finally succumbed to the bay. Its remains lie on the bottom of the bay, so use caution if wading.

Launch site at Barbour's Hill

vs

Photo Courtesy of Reese Lukei, Jr.

Osprey (Pandion haliaetus)

Reese F. Lukei, Jr.

The osprey, commonly called the "fish hawk," is a spring and summer resident in the Hampton Roads region of Virginia. It is the only member of the family Pandionidae, and is found on every continent except the Antarctic. *Pandion* is thought to mean "bone crusher" and *haliaetus* means "fish eagle."

Osprey are large raptors measuring 21 to 26 inches from head to tail and have a wing span of 59 to 67 inches. Like other birds of prey, the female is larger than the male. Males weigh from 2 lbs. 2 oz. to 3 lbs 2 oz and females 2 lbs. 8 oz to 3 lbs. 9 oz. They can live as long as 26 years, but 8 to 10 years is more normal. The immature osprey has red-orange eyes and white speckles on its upper body feathers, while the adult has yellow eyes and solid brownish black upper body feathers.

The fish hawk's diet consists almost exclusively of fish and eels, gathered from both fresh and salt water. It hunts by flying 30 - 100 feet above the water surface, hovers briefly when it sights a fish, dives with wings beating and plunges feet first with a big splash sometimes going completely under water. It rises with powerful wings that allow it to break the surface of the water, gives a shudder to rid its feathers of water, and heads for its favorite feeding perch. The feet have three special adaptations that help hold slippery fish: long and strongly curved talons, sharp spicules in the palm, and an outer toe that can be positioned forward or backward. The osprey always flys with the head of the fish forward.

Photo Courtesy of Reese Lukei, Jr.

In Hampton Roads, Virginia and northeast North Carolina the osprey begin to arrive by late February from their wintering grounds as far south as Venezuela. Immediately upon their return they begin their search for a nest site, and once its location is agreed upon, construction begins. Older pairs return to the same site year after year. The nest is a bulky affair about four feet in diameter built of sticks and lined with marsh grasses and sometimes pine boughs. It is always in the open and usually on top of dead trees, channel markers, utility poles and other man-made structures such as lighting structures at ball fields. They bring all kinds of non-natural items to the nest such as rope, plastic objects, balls, construction materials, and fishing line. Tragically, these man-made pieces can be fatal if the birds consume or become entangled in them.

Osprey breed at the age of three years. The female lays 2 to 4 white eggs with light to heavy brown markings. She incubates the eggs for 32-33 days. The young fledge in 52-54 days after hatching. Adults fiercely defend their nests and will dive-bomb intruders. The resident osprey have usually migrated south by mid-August, so those seen in southeastern Virginia and northeastern North Carolina during the fall are migrating from areas further north.

The Chesapeake Bay watershed is thought to have the largest concentration of osprey in the world which makes them easy to observe throughout our region. Once considered a threatened specie in Virginia (1978), its population today has significantly recovered because of reintroduction efforts and public support. The osprey is now protected under our wildlife laws just as are other species.

The sight of osprey over our local waters is now quite common. The next time you are paddling and see a large shadow over the water, look up and see if you can recognize the "bone-crushing fish-eagle."

Note: The migratory bird season occurs from October through March. Each year the Virginia Department of Game and Inland Fisheries establishes the hunting seasons on waterfowl and game birds. These dates fall between September and December. The duck blinds seen in the bay are assigned to hunters who are required to get a waterfowl blind license. For more information visit www.dgif.virginia.gov/hunting.

The Bald Eagle (Haliaeetus leucocephalus)
Reese F. Lukei, Jr.

Eagles inhabit every continent except Antarctica. Worldwide there are 59 species of eagles classified into four groups: sea or fish eagles such as the bald eagle, booted eagles like the golden eagle, snake eagles found mostly in Africa, and giant forest eagles like the harpy eagle of Central America.

Two eagles are widely found in the United States. The golden eagle is located mostly in the western states, but is actually native to the mountains of Virginia. It is occasionally seen during the winter months in the coastal areas of the Eastern Shore of Virginia. The world-wide range is throughout the Western Hemisphere, Europe and Asia. Two specie of sea eagles, the white-tailed and steller's, are rare visitors to Alaska's coasts and islands.

The bald eagle is found only in North America. Its name is derived from the old English word "balde" which means white. The scientific name *Haliaeetus leucocephalus* means "fish eagle with white head." Bald eagles generally take five years to mature and achieve the familiar white head and tail. Young (immature) bald eagles are dark brown with some white speckling. As they age during their second and third years, they have a varied amount of white feathers, especially on their underside and they are then referred to as white-bellied.

Golden eagles and bald eagles are approximately the same size and are the largest raptors (birds of prey) in North America. The female is larger than the male, a characteristic common in raptors. The female usually weighs 8 to 12 pounds and the male about 7 to 10 pounds. The wingspan is 7 to 8 feet. Bald eagles that live in our northern regions are usually larger than those in the southernmost parts of the U.S. In the wild they can live up to 30 years and in captivity up to 40.

Bald eagles are thought to have the best eyesight of any animal, having up to eight times the resolving power of the human eye. The retina has two focusing foveae (human eyes have only one) which allows them to use both eyes together (binocular vision like humans) for telescopic viewing, or each eye independently (monocular vision) for up close viewing. They see in color.

Bald eagles mate for life and can produce young for over 20 years. In Virginia they usually lay one to three off-white eggs in January and incubate them for about 35 days. The young usually fledge (fly) in 10 to 13 weeks, then spend another 4 to 6 weeks near the nest, where the adults continue to feed them. The nest is usually in a tall loblolly pine, but they may use a wide variety of tall trees. A nest may be used by the same pair for many years, can be up to 8 feet wide and 12 feet deep, and weigh over 1,000 pounds.

The diet of bald eagles varies, but consists largely of fish that they locate from a tree perch along the edge of a lake or riverbank. Scavengers rather than hunters, they feed mostly on sick or injured prey. They will eat carrion and take advantage of any opportunity.

In the state of Virginia, annual surveys of the Center for Conservation Biology at the College of William and Mary produced the data below concerning recent breeding populations and fledged young.

Year	Pairs	Fledged	Year	Pairs	Fledged
2001	313	466	2005	429	657
2002	329	501	2006	469	705
2003	371	454	2007	550	730
2004	401	612			

Like many other species, the Bald Eagle population was severely diminished by our use of persistent pesticides like DDT. In 1972 there were 32 pair in Virginia who produced 18 young. As a result of federal and Virginia protection measures, good land management practices and constant monitoring, the population today has recovered significantly. In 1994 the federal and Virginia status of the Bald Eagle was changed from endangered to threatened.

More and more, paddlers on our local waterways are reporting eagle sightings. This symbol of our nation is truly magnificent whether seen from land or water. We can all feel fortunate to have on our life lists "the fish eagle with white head."

Bio: Reese F. Lukei, Jr. has been a U.S. Fish and Wildlife Service volunteer since 1974, and a volunteer research associate at the Center for Conservation Biology at the College of William and Mary since it was founded in 1991. He is licensed by the Commonwealth of Virginia, the U.S. Fish and Wildlife Service and U.S. Geological Survey to trap and band raptors and has banded over 15,000 hawks, falcons, eagles and owls.

Section 8. (I) False Cape Landing to (J) Wash Woods, 1½ miles

From False Cape Landing it's fun to paddle along the edges of the cove before entering Back Bay. Being somewhat protected from the wind, it provides a safe haven for an abundance of wildlife. Once you have entered Back Bay, go south and around the point. On the other side you will see Wash Woods. To take out, look for the boat house and the boat dock leading out into the water. To extend your trip, continue south and circle around Little Ball Island. Otters are sometimes seen playing on the back side of the island.

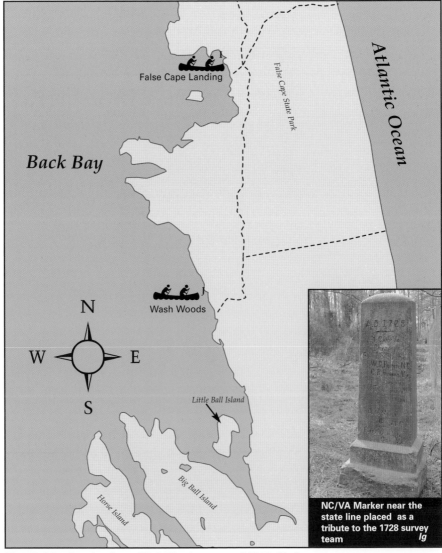

False Cape Landing

False Cape State Park

Atlantic Ocean

Back Bay

N

W — E

S

Wash Woods

Little Ball Island

Big Ball Island

Horse Island

NC/VA Marker near the state line placed as a tribute to the 1728 survey team   *lg*

Map 18: False Cape Landing to Wash Woods   *© Vickie Shufer*

Submerged Aquatic Vegetation (SAV)

One of the delightful aspects of canoeing and kayaking is the ability to see what's beneath the boat (if the water is clear enough). Drifting on a wind-driven course, it's fun to watch the small minnows that dart among the underwater vegetation. At low tide, SAV can be seen on the sand flats at the edge of the marsh.

Submerged aquatic vegetation is an important resource in the bay waters. Wild celery, widgeon grass, coontail, milfoil and sago pondweed are among the SAV plants found in Back Bay. They provide food and habitat for a number of fish and wildlife that live in or around the bay. While fish and other aquatic animals may feed directly on the SAV, they in turn become food for osprey, herons, egrets, ducks, swans and geese who are often seen fishing in these vegetation beds. Studies have shown that when SAVs are high, the dabbling duck population increases.

In order for SAV to grow, water must be somewhat clear to allow light to penetrate for photosynthesis. Dredging, motorboats and jet skis contribute to stirring up the water and inhibiting light penetration. The presence of SAV is an indicator of the health of the bay.

Watermilfoil

Redhead Grass

Wild Celery

Sago Pondweed

Aquatic Wildlife

Aquatic wildlife in Back Bay has gone through changes over the years as a result of decreasing salinity and the decline in aquatic vegetation. White perch is one of the most common sport fish found here. Aquatic wildlife also includes blue-spotted sunfish, bluegill, silversides, pumpkinseed, catfish, shad, herring, carp and eels. The shallow waters act as a nursery for small fish, offering protection from larger predators. A seine net or dip net can be used to sample the waters for specimens to get a close-up look at what lives in the bay.

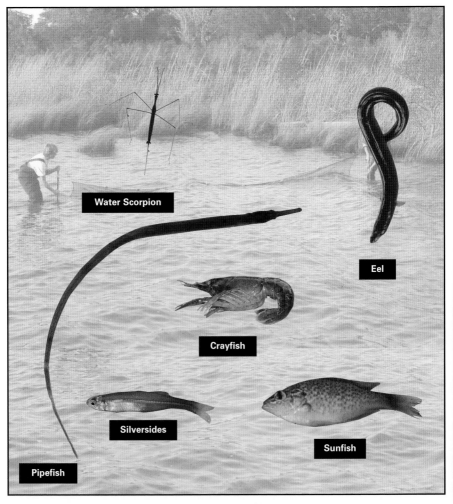

If there is magic on this planet, it is contained in water.   Loren Eiseley

Up to the Knees in Mud

Those who have strayed into lower water levels have found getting out of parts of Back Bay very annoying. The 18th century Back Bay paddling experience of William Byrd as part of the VA/NC state line survey team may sound familiar to the paddler of the 21st century.

> *... we embarked ourselves...to find a Passage round the North End of the [Knotts] Island. We found this Navigation very difficult, by reason of the Continued Shoals, and often stuck fast aground; for tho' the Sound spreads many miles, yet it is in most places extremely Shallow, and requires a Skilful Pilot to steer even a Canoe safe over it. ...At a distance we descry'd Several Islands to the Northward of us, the largest of which goes by the Name of Cedar Island... we rowed up an arm of the Sound, call'd the Back-Bay, til we came to the Head of it. There we were stoppt by a Miry Pocoson full half a Mile in Breadth, thro' which we were oblid'd to daggle on foot, plungeing now and then, tho' we pickt our Way, up to the Knees in Mud. At the end of this Charming walk we gained the Terra Firma of Princess Anne County.*
>
> ~ William Byrd II, March 8, 1728, somewhere in Back Bay

Paddling Tip

If you should have an out-of-boat experience and find yourself knee deep in mud and unable to pull your legs out, drop to your knees and use the lower part of your legs as a snowshoe to walk on the mud.

Students exploring the marsh

Tracks in the Mud

A number of animals visit the bays and waterways each day to feed. Though the animal itself is not always seen, its presence is revealed by the tracks left behind in the mud or wet sand. When the water is low, look for tracks along the edges, or sometimes, if the water is clear enough, beneath the water on the bottom of the bay.

Bird Tracks

Birds generally show three toes that point forward and one that points backward. The feet of ducks show webbing between the toes.

Mammal Tracks

Most mammals have paws with five toes on each foot. Fox and bobcat show only four toes – the fifth toe is too small to leave an impression. Deer, pigs and horses have hoofs. Nutria and otter sometimes show webbing on the back paws as well as a tail drag. Otter tracks are more round than nutria and leave distinct toe marks, almost in a straight line. Raccoon tracks have long fingerlike marks.

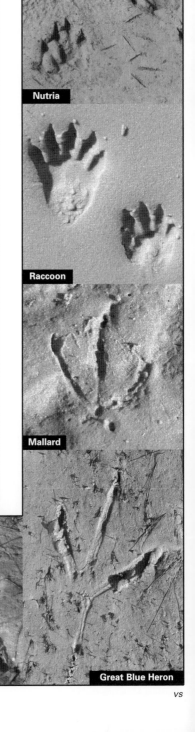

Nutria

Raccoon

Mallard

Otter

Great Blue Heron

vs

False Cape State Park

South of Back Bay National Wildlife Refuge, sandwiched between Back Bay on the west and the Atlantic Ocean on the east is False Cape State Park. It is a mile-wide barrier spit that can only be accessed by boat, hiking or biking (the interior trail through the refuge is closed from November 1 through March 31). Groups can schedule a ride to the park on the Terra Gator, a specially designed vehicle that can be taken on the beach. There is also a tram that is operated by the Back Bay Restoration Foundation that transports individuals from Little Island Park through the wildlife refuge to the state park from April 1 through October 31. A two hour layover in the Barbour Hill area

vs

allows visitors to explore the park or walk to the beach or bay. Call 757-426-3643 for information on tram tours. An environmental education center in the Wash Woods area accommodates groups for ecological studies for day trips or overnight use. Primitive camping is available year round on the bay side or oceanfront. Reservations are required. For information, call 757-426-3657.

vs

False Cape State Park consists of 4321 acres of marshes, maritime forests, swamps, sand dunes and almost 6 miles of beachfront extending to the North Carolina line. Its name comes from the resemblance of the land mass to Cape Henry, luring boats in to shallow waters. A thriving community called Wash Woods once existed between the primary dune and Back Bay. A church was built from wood that washed ashore during a shipwreck. All that remains today is the church steeple and a graveyard.

Photo Courtesy of Joe Thornton

Gun Clubs of Wash Woods and False Cape

Before the shifting sands and storms of the 1920s, Wash Woods community included many farmers, fishermen, and hunting guides. As the community's residents slipped away, small tracts of land became available which were bought as gunning clubs and weekend retreats. By county law, no club could be within 500 yards of another. At least six clubs were operating prior to 1924, but by the year's end in 1924, over two dozen private buildings were erected as hunting retreats.

In 1966 when the state of Virginia bought land along the south Atlantic coast in Virginia Beach, several hunt clubs or gun clubs or the former sites of such became the property of what is now known as False Cape State Park. One unusual clubhouse was the Newport News Gunning Club. Originally known as the Ball Island Gunning Club, this land included Big Ball and Little Ball Islands located southwest of the Wash Woods landing. It was a four-sided building completely covered by slate, probably owing to the owner's connections in West Virginia. Mr. James Branch's Guyan River Coal Company may have had the slate mined and shipped by rail to Norfolk or Virginia Beach. The building is no longer in existence, however you can still find pieces of slate buried in the sand as a reminder of times gone by.

The park superintendent's house was once part of the weekend getaway of David Newby of Norfolk and was called the Newby Hunting Lodge. The old Swan Club, originally named the Vir-Mar Gunning Club in 1920 and then the Norfolk Hunt Club, is now the Environmental Education Center for the park and allows overnight guests by reservation

Swan Decoys

for purposes of environmental studies. In the 1940s the Goat Hill Gunning Club was located south of Wash Woods. Owner Charlie Waterfield acted as hunting guide for his overnight or week-long guests. The property was sold to two gentlemen from Newport News, with Charlie acting as caretaker, then was acquired by the state. Mr. Waterfield, during his lifetime devotion to waterfowling, carved many decoys which are highly sought-after by collectors.

The many island clubs included the Cedar Island Club, originally built in the 1880s by John Williams. Today, paddlers will discover that the once large island is actually two islands, Little Cedar and Big Cedar. This property was acquired in 1977 by Virginia to be part of False Cape State Park. For an excellent detailed history of all of the clubs and individuals associated with them, the authors encourage the reading of *Gun Clubs and Decoys of Back Bay and Currituck Sound* by Archie Johnson and Bud Coppedge. For more information, contact the Atlantic Wildfowl Heritage Museum in Virginia Beach, VA at 757-437-8432.

Big Cedar Island

False Cape Memories

Many locals still remember "the good old days" when they could drive cars or trucks down the beach, find a comfortable spot, build a campfire, and spend the night. Others went a step farther. They brought in construction materials and built houses. It was a squatter's para-

Photo from the collection of Gary Koehling

dise. They were called the "weekenders" by those who lived there. The permanent residents lived on the bay side while the "weekenders" lived on the ocean side. They didn't own the land, they just squatted.

The state began acquiring land in the late 1960s. In 1973 the U.S. Fish and Wildlife Service banned traffic through the refuge except for those who had a home on the Currituck Banks and worked in Virginia. They were issued permits that allowed them to travel between their homes and work places.

The weekenders had no choice but to leave. Since they did not own the land, they had the choice of taking their houses with them or leaving them behind, which is what most of them did. Not only did they leave their houses behind, but many of the furnishings as well. Today all that is left are memories and a few memorabilia where their houses once stood.

Open Range Livestock

Until the mid 1930's, cattle and pigs were free to graze in the forests and swamps in this coastal area. Since colonial times, farmers would keep a few animals penned until they were needed, but otherwise they ran wild. By the time open range grazing was banned, the pigs had found their place in the forests and marshes. When the state bought the land that is now False Cape State Park, the people moved out but some left their animals behind. Descendants of these animals became feral and continue to survive in the marshes and woods, digging up the soil while looking for roots and grubs.

Paul Shufer

Part 4

Virginia Beach Oceanfront

Virginia Beach Oceanfront

The thought of paddling along the edge of a continent is truly exciting. That opportunity awaits in Virginia Beach. The Atlantic Ocean to the east and Chesapeake Bay to the north give paddlers different launching opportunities and varieties of wave experiences. For those wanting a calmer paddle, try the bayfront. The city has about 38 miles of beaches and bayfront with 7.1 linear miles of ocean public beaches: North Beach, Resort Beach, Croatan, Camp Pendleton. While access is available at city public access areas, the authors urge utmost caution when paddling in open water. Those not experienced in ocean paddling are encouraged to take classes and gain experience. The authors accept no responsibility for any damages due to launching, landing or paddling in any body of water. It is wise to check on any new legislation regarding launching kayaks off the beach. See page 175 or www.vbgov.com.

If time, visit the Virginia Beach Boardwalk, 3 miles long, or 40 blocks, for walking, skating or bicycling. Landscaped as a linear park, it has restrooms and benches for ocean gazing and peoplewatching. Old-fashioned lampposts recall an earlier time of the 1888 wooden boardwalk. From the end of May to early September, visitors enjoy Beach Street USA, a diverse array of street performers from 17th to 25th Streets along Atlantic Avenue.

Location

Virginia Beach's Oceanfront is bordered south by the North Carolina state line and north by the Chesapeake Bay. Paddling trips described here are Camp Pendleton/Croatan Beach about one mile south of Rudee Inlet to Cape Henry to the north and then west to Chesapeake Bay beach at First Landing State Park.

Access Points

A. Croatan Beach
B. Owl Creek Boat Ramp
C. Resort area – 2nd Street to 42nd Street
D. 42nd Street to 89th Street
E. 89th Street
F. First Landing State Park Campground

Oceanfront

*Photo courtesy of
Virginia Beach Tourism*

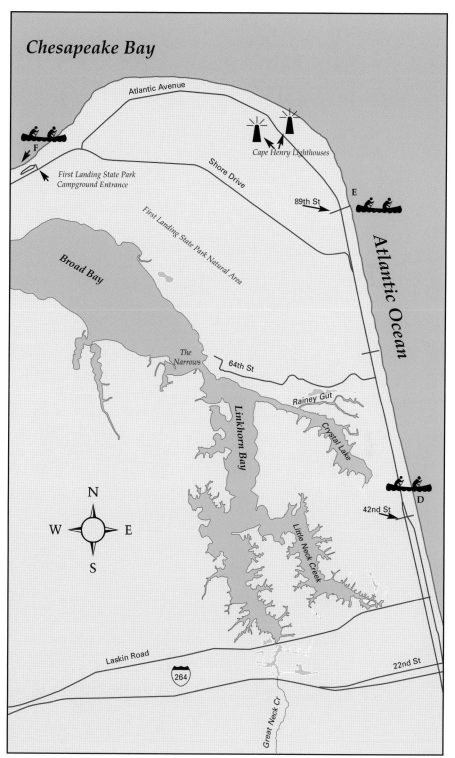

Chesapeake Bay

Atlantic Avenue

F

First Landing State Park
Campground Entrance

Shore Drive

Cape Henry Lighthouses

First Landing State Park Natural Area

89th St

E

Broad Bay

The
Narrows

64th St

Rainey Gut

Crystal Lake

Linkhorn Bay

Atlantic Ocean

N
W   E
S

42nd St

D

Little Neck Creek

Laskin Road

264

22nd St

Great Neck Cr

Map 20: Oceanfront from Croatan Beach to 42nd Street

© Vickie Shufer

Access Points
A. Croatan Beach
Directions: From I-264 go south on Pacific Avenue. After crossing the Rudee Inlet bridge, go about ½ miles and turn east on Croatan Drive. Go almost to the end and turn south on Vanderbilt and continue to the public parking area at the end. There is a parking fee between Memorial Day weekend and Labor Day weekend. Follow the wooden boardwalk across the dunes to the beach. Public restrooms are available as well as an outdoor shower and changing room.

B. Owl Creek Boat Ramp
Directions: From the resort strip, drive south on Pacific Avenue. Where Pacific Avenue crosses Rudee Inlet at the Rudee Bridge, Pacific Avenue changes names to become General Booth Blvd. Travel less than a mile to the free boat ramp and parking area. Extra parking is across the street. There are portable restrooms on site but no fresh water. Open year round, dawn to dusk.

C. Resort area, 2nd Street to 42nd Street
Pull into 2nd Street as far as you can and off load, then drive to the municipal 4th Street parking lot. This method is usually the easiest since on-street parking is metered by the hour. Launch from the beach and head north. The beach at 2nd Street is not as crowded as some of the other potential launch sites in the resort area. Launching from this beach spot will keep the paddler away from the dangerous rock jetties at Rudee Inlet.

Important note: There is a city code against launching or landing here and from Rudee Inlet to 42nd Street from the Friday before Memorial Day through the Monday following the Labor Day weekend during the hours of 10 a.m. - 4 p.m. on weekdays and 10 a.m. - 6 p.m., weekends. For details see page 175.

General Booth Boulevard
General Booth Boulevard was named for Adjunct General Paul Milton Booth, commander of the Virginia National Guard, the Virginia Air National Guard and the Virginia Defense Force between 1960 and 1970. The position of Adjunct General is a governor appointed position first established in 1794. After the devastating Ash Wednesday Storm battered the coastline in March of 1962, General Booth brought troops to Virginia Beach to protect property, prevent looting and assist in the massive clean-up efforts. In appreciation, the City of Virginia Beach named the boulevard which opened in 1963 in his honor.

D. 42nd Street to 89th Street

Directions: From I-264, go north on Pacific Avenue which becomes Atlantic Avenue at Cavalier Drive. The distinctive hotel on the hill is the Cavalier Hotel located on 42nd Street overlooking the oceanfront. This landmark locates the start of the beach area at 42nd Street that is not regulated by city code (as of this publication date) concerning the launching and landing of kayaks. Do not launch

Walkway to beach at 89th St.   lg

directly on the beach in front of the Cavalier. Look for streets that offer public access to the beach, offload, and park where you can legally.

Remember: Wear a spray skirt when ocean paddling. Launching off this wide part of the beach can be challenging on a rough water day, so err on the side of caution and if conditions are not good, go to Owl Creek and explore the inner, protected waterways there.

E. 89th Street

At the intersection of Shore Drive and Atlantic Avenue, turn north to remain on Atlantic Avenue and follow the numbered streets until you reach 89th Street. There is limited public parking from 42nd Street to 89th Street in the residential area and in some places along the feeder road. Be courteous to private property owners and park only where allowed. The easiest way to access the ocean is to turn east on one of the numbered streets, drive to the end and unload and then park your vehicle. It helps to have a partner to stay with the gear while parking. Launching from this beach spot will keep the paddler away from the dangerous rock jetties at Rudee Inlet.

89th Street Walkway   *Photo by Michelle Finck*

Parking at 89th Street is always a challenge. The access at the end of 89th Street is a lovely walk through a green tunnel of live oaks to the beach. The shaded walkway is a glimpse at old Virginia Beach and the last remnants of a maritime forest that used to occupy the Atlantic waterfront. The carry to the beach is a long one but worth it.

(F) First Landing State Park Campground

Directions: Drive north on Atlantic Avenue until you come to the intersection of Shore Drive and go west about 4½ miles until you come to a stop light. Turn north into the campground. Stop at the contact station to get a day pass and pay the parking fee (Call 757-412-2320 for current fees). Park in the large parking lot on the left. A wooden boardwalk leads from the western end of the parking lot to the beach.

Facilities: At the western end of the parking lot is a long building that was originally built by the Civilian Conservation Corps in the 1930s. Today it houses the park offices, camp store, restrooms and the Chesapeake Bay Center.

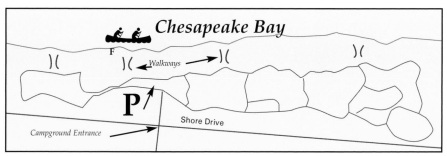

Map 21: First Landing State Park Campground

Chesapeake Bay Center

The Chesapeake Bay Center is a nature-based ecotourism information center for Virginia Beach and a designated Chesapeake Bay Gateways Regional Information Center. It contains environmental exhibits, three aquariums, classroom space, a wet lab and touch tank developed by the Virginia Marine Science Museum. It is open 9:00 a.m. to 5:00 p.m., closed only on Christmas and New Year's Day. For more information, call 757-412-2316.

Chesapeake Bay Center

vs

Paddling Sections

1. **(A) Croatan Beach to Rudee Inlet or points north** – mileage variable
2. **(B) Owl Creek Boat Ramp/Rudee Inlet** – mileage variable
3. **(C) Resort area, 2nd Street to (D) 42nd Street (Paddle this during off-season only)** – 3 miles
4. **(D) 42nd Street to (E) 89th Street** – 3 miles
5. **(E) 89th Street to (F) First Landing State Park** – 3½ miles

Section 1. (A) Croatan Beach to Rudee Inlet or points north – mileage variable

Launching off this sandy beach can be ideal on a calm day. Pick your weather and if the ocean is too rough, drive to Owl Creek and explore the two "lakes" and some of the small backwaters.

If the day is a good one then try your skills at ocean paddling if you

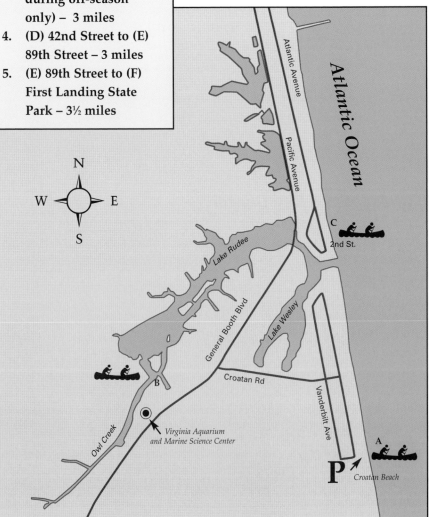

Map 22: Croatan Beach to 2nd Street

© Vickie Shufer

110

have the proper experience and training. We must, however, caution inexperienced paddlers not to take risks. The waves can be extremely dangerous. This is a surfer's beach and a paddler's beach, so be prepared to give way to board users. We do suggest that if you launch here, use this as your take-out as well. Enjoy a paddle along the beach in either direction and avoid the rock jetty at Rudee Inlet.

The scenery is as you would expect in a developed beach environment with beautiful homes and a stunning ocean view. Should you decide to paddle into Rudee Inlet, be very cautious as this is a high traffic zone for motorized boats, large and small. The rock jetty and the refracted waves interior to the jetty area pose particular risk which can damage people and equipment. If you are an experienced paddler with surfing and self-rescue skills, this area can be fun and challenging.

Marina and boat docks at Lake Rudee,
Lake Holly in background

Photo Courtesy of Virginia Beach Tourism

Section 2. (B) Owl Creek Boat Ramp – mileage variable

The only public access into this paddling section is Owl Creek Boat Ramp located on General Booth Boulevard northwest of the Virginia Aquarium and Marine Science Center. This area of Virginia Beach is about as populated as it can get, so the natural areas that are visible to the south are appreciated. A relaxing time to paddle is right before sunset when the water is usually calm and there are fewer motorboats. Motorized craft don't usually hang around in this area, but as a paddler you night want to explore some of the tiny inlets. This is a quiet water area good for birding and fishing. This would be a good spot to hone one's kayak fishing skills.

This larger body of water is called Lake Rudee even though it is an inlet connecting to the Atlantic. There are a couple of small creeks to explore to the west side of Rudee: Snail Creek to the southwest known for the high concentration of marsh periwinkle snails that attach themselves to the cordgrass and Getaway Creek to the northwest. These creek names are not found on any map although a handful of natives who paddle here know these names.

The creek that is alongside the Virginia Aquarium is the actual Owl Creek. This is a short but pleasant paddle and the paddler will see the outdoor aviary and at the end of the waterway, an amusement park. Salt meadow hay is the thin-bladed hay-like native grass growing along the banks.

Closer to the Rudee Inlet Bridge, the area is crowded with waterfront homes, condos, waterfront restaurants, docks and piers with private and commercial fishing boats. The whale-watching boats leave from the docks in this area. Use caution when paddling under the bridge as the larger boats may not see you coming. We recommend taking the water to the south side of the bridge to stay out of boat traffic. The other cove, called Lake Wesley, is located to the southeast of the Rudee Inlet Bridge. In the summer it is possible to observe tropical fish that probably got off track from the Gulf Stream as it swings close to Virginia Beach. Fishing and crabbing are good here.

Boat from Virginia Aquarium on Owl Creek

Owl Creek/Rudee History

A U.S. Army Corps of Engineers report suggests that an opening at Rudee may have been in place as early as 1585 (Everts, Battley, and Gibson, 1983). A French map dated 1781 shows a sizeable inlet and indicates Owl Creek as one of three coves interior to the inlet. These probably represent what we know as Owl Creek, Lake Rudee, Lake Wesley and Lake Holly (now a pair of storm water retention ponds). At the whim of shifting sands, storm and tidal action, Rudee Inlet eventually became a small, winding tidal swale and drained a relatively small marsh. The much-changed and enlarged Lake Rudee, Owl Creek, Lake Wesley and Rudee Inlet of today supports a vital tourism asset for commercial and deep-sea fishing, recreational boating, the Virginia Aquarium and Marine Science Center, restaurants as well as home sites and amenities for residents. It is the only direct access to the ocean from the resort area and as an open inlet, it is an important component in the City's beach erosion control program.

In 1927 a concrete flume/culvert was constructed by the Virginia Department of Transportation across the low spot in an effort to curb the natural movement of the sandy drain area and to support a concrete road that would bridge the oceanfront to the south (an area now called Croatan). The hand operated wooden sluice, the flume and road were destroyed in the August 1933 Hurricane. Pieces of that concrete street and flume washed inland as the Rudee Inlet opened once more due to storm action (Henry, 2007). During the 1940s it is known that the inlet could walked across or waded across at varoius times and tides. In 1952/53, the Town (with cooperation from the state) mined sand from Lake Wesley and the marsh (now the larger Lake Rudee) to replenish the developing resort area. In order to get the dredge mobilized for the sand mining, two short jetties were built to stabilize the mouth of the inlet.

After the removal of 3,500,000 cubic yards of sand for beachfront replenishment, what remained was an open water estuary where the marsh and old lake beds were. The development that followed along the newly created waterfront property placed many demands on the land and water and particularly on the stabilization of the inlet itself. Since that time many changes and structural improvements to the inlet have occurred (City of Virginia Beach, 2002).

The origin of the name of the inlet remains a study point. There are maps of early Virginia Beach which spell the name "Rudy" and "Roede." What the actual story is, we may never know.

Owl Creek/Rudee Inlet to the ocean and beyond

Today it is possible to paddle directly into the ocean or into a jetty-braced area on the south immediately before the ocean entrance. This can be the bailout area if the waves are too rough for a smooth ride. Going into the ocean here is not recommended for open canoes or inexperienced kayakers. The currents are severe and the swells deceiving. Know your limits. Also know that this is a busy inlet with motorboats large and small sharing the same entrance to the Atlantic Ocean. The rocky entrance can be dangerous. However, if you do decide to paddle into the ocean, you will be rewarded with a view of the resort skyline from a vantage point seen by few.

Owl Creek Boat Ramp   *vs*

Virginia Aquarium and Marine Science Center

Plan to visit the Virginia Aquarium and Marine Science Museum located next to the boat launch facility. This science facility with many exhibits, aquariums and hands-on programs is dedicated to increasing the public's knowledge about the local marine environment. The museum is involved in active research and rescue efforts concerning marine mammals and sea turtles. It also sponsors whale-watching and dolphin-watching trips that depart daily out of Rudee Inlet during appropriate months. For more information, email Fish@VirginiaAquarium.com, call 757-385-FISH (3474), or visit www.virginiaaquarium.com.

Section 3. Resort area, (C) 2nd Street to (D) 42nd Street (Paddle this during off-season only) – 3 miles

This access site is convenient to parking and restaurant facilities. It's fairly easy to launch here due to the bit of protection by the rock jetties at Rudee Inlet which are to the north of this site. Launching here is much safer than paddling across or through Rudee Inlet. Surfers and swimmers also use the beach so caution and politeness are a must. There are often those who believe the beach is there just for them when it can be shared safely if we're all careful. Do check weather and waves. Wear a spray skirt when paddling in the ocean. Head north to avoid Rudee Inlet and enjoy the waterfront of Virginia Beach. Launching and landing here and north to 42nd

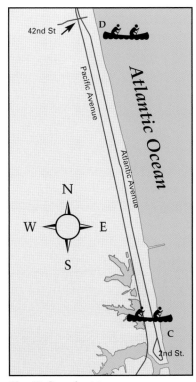

Map 23: Oceanfront to 2nd St to 42nd St *vs*

Street are in violation of city code unless paddling in the off-season. See the note under "Access Sites" for the 2nd Street beach, the description of the resort season and check the city's website for updates: www.vbgov.com. Also see page 175, Appendix A – City Code for Launching Boats in Virginia Beach.

Perils of the Sea

In the early 1940s, German U-boats placed mines that sank ships just off the Virginia Beach coast. Older residents remember when there was a wartime curfew with lights out so the shoreline was not so visible. This coast was the welcome shoreline in 1607 when the first permanent English colony was about to be established.

The Robert C. Tuttle hit by magnetic mines left by the U701 German submarine. The burning ship was struck in June 1942 offshore between 21st and 24th Streets.

Photo Courtesy of the Old Coast Guard Station

Section 4. (D) 42nd Street to (E) 89th Street – 3 miles

Heading north along the Atlantic shoreline, the paddler is never out of sight of the many waterfront dwellings of the "North End." This is a popular place to live, visit, or recreate. The take-out at 89th Street can be seen as the fencing at Fort Story comes into view. There is a tiny bit of maritime forest green that can be glimpsed from the water and this marks the walkway back to 89th Street.

This is a good spot to watch for dolphins. Once in the ocean, you won't have to paddle far to see them but do be patient and don't chase them. Let them approach you. They can grow up to 12 feet long and weigh up to 1,400 pounds. To our knowledge, no one has ever been harmed here by these wonderful creatures. They are curious and definitely fun loving. One August day one of your authors was rewarded by seeing small children body surfing alongside small dolphins. Both were squealing with what appeared to be joyful noises.

Vickie paddling along oceanfront   *Photo by Susan Heyburn*

And still I break up through the skin of awareness a thousand times a day, as dolphins burst through seas, and dive again, and rise, and dive.
                    Annie Dillard, *An American Childhood*

Paddling With the Dolphins

Summer is an active time for the Atlantic bottenose dolphin along the east coast, including the lower Chesapeake Bay. They are sociable animals and travel in groups called pods, made up of seven or more animals of varying ages and gender. They belong to a group of marine mammals which includes whales, dolphins and porpoises They use clicking sounds that allow them to "see" with their ears through echolocation. They also appear to communicate with other members of their pod by producing whistling sounds. (www.chesapeakebay.net). Rubbing your hand on the side of the boat or whistling can sometimes attract the dolphins to you, who will often leap into the air or swim under your boat before continuing on.

Following is an account from an early experience:

I had entered the water and was only about waist deep, still close to shore. I playfully started whistling and calling to the dolphins to come play with me. Suddenly, right in front of me was a whole pod of dolphins coming toward me. They looked huge. As they swam around me, they were so close I could almost reach out and touch them. And then, just as quickly as they had appeared they were gone.

From the journal of Vickie Shufer

Photo Courtesy of Virginia Beach Tourism

Shorebirds

Shorebirds are a common sight while paddling along the oceanfront. Fish swimming in off-shore waters attract fish-eating birds. Brown pelicans have become numerous since the early 1980s, and catch their fish by diving into the water and using their pouches as a dip net to scoop up fish. Water is drained from the pouch before the fish is swallowed.

Brown Pelican

Gulls and terns are the most numerous and can be observed resting on the beach or flying overhead, while others may be floating offshore. Gulls are sociable birds who colonize at low tide to rest and feed. They patrol the beaches, cleaning up dead and decaying debris. The beak is blunt and slightly hooked on the end.

Laughing Gull

Terns are smaller, close relatives of the gulls and often mingle with them. Their food consists mainly of fish. The long, pointed beak is used as a spear for catching fish which they catch by diving into the water.

Black skimmers leave a trail across the water as its extended lower beak cuts through the surface. The bill has a special adaptation for catching fish. A strong hinge connects the upper beak with the forehead. The longer, lower bill can move freely up and down as it comes in contact with fish in the water.

Black Skimmer

On the beach, from the low tide line to the high tide line, numerous shorebirds can be seen running back and forth with the tides, probing into the sand with their pointed beaks for burrowing animals that live just below the tide line. Groups of sandpipers, plovers and turnstones travel together in loosely formed colonies.

Sanderlings and seagull

Section 5. (E) 89th Street to (F) First Landing State Park Campground – 3½ miles

If you are an experienced paddler and want to head north you can round Cape Henry and enter the Chesapeake Bay. The paddling distance from the public beach heading north, then west around Cape Henry to the campground on the Chesapeake Bay at First Landing State Park is about 3 ½ miles. Paddlers are not allowed to beach boats on any part of Fort Story, a U.S. Army base. Continue until the state park property is in view. Long boardwalks that are the visible landmarks. Look for the third boardwalk from the east for your take out. There is a wide boardwalk that brings you to the parking lot, restrooms and other amenities.

Walkway crossing the dunes at First Landing State Park   *vs*

Boardwalk at First Landing State Park   *vs*

Paddling to the Lesner Bridge at the mouth of the Lynnhaven River from the northern boundary of the park is about 3 miles. Check the tides carefully if you plan to round Cape Henry. Tides here can be very powerful so be careful and don't over-estimate your skill level. Paddle on an incoming tide for safety. An alternate access point is near the Lynnhaven Fishing Pier.

Shoreline History

Spanish sailors probably spotted the shoreline of today's Virginia Beach in the 1500s. In the winter of 1585-86, the English explorers John White and Thomas Harriot landed on our splendid shores and spent a little time among the Chesepian Indians, who lived in the area we now know as Norfolk, Chesapeake, Portsmouth and Virginia Beach. White draws an interesting map showing the Indian towns of Apasus and Skicoak plotted not too far from Cape Henry, possibly on what are today's Lynnhaven River, the Elizabeth River or the Nansemond River. While to the English it was a "New World," the Indians they encountered came from ancestors that had lived in Tidewater for more than a thousand years. The inquisitive scholar Harriot learned a lot of the Carolina Indians' Algonquian language, which is probably a different dialect from the Chesepians or Powhatans. He memorized from the Indians the names of plants, places, villages, various bodies of water and anything else he needed to use as a reference. The Chesapeake Bay was known as *Chisapeak*, "the great salt bay" (Rountree, 1989) or by other accounts, *Chesopean*, "the great shellfish bay." This "great shellfish" was the oyster, in those days growing to the size of a dinner plate. Most scholars agree that the Chesepian Indians had been eradicated by the Powhatans before the arrival of the first permanent white settlers in 1607. In a report, Ralph Lane mentions a voyage to the area in 1585-86, but we are left without knowing the exact route taken from the settlement in North Carolina to the land of the Chesepians (quoted from *The Roanoke Voyages 1584-1590*, edited by David Beers Quinn).

> To the Northwarde our furthest discourie was to the Chesepians, distant from Roanoak about 130 miles, the passage to it was very shallow and most dangerous, by reason of the breadth of the sound, and the little succor that vpon any flawe was there to be had.

> But the Territorie and soyle of the Chesepians (being distant fifteene miles from the shoar) was for pleasantness of seate, for temperature of Climate, for fertilitie of soyle, and for the commoditie of the Sea, besides multitude of beares (being an excellent good victual, with great woods of Sassafras, and Wall nut trees) is not to be excelled by any other whatsoeuer.

In a letter dated December 30, 1586 to Sir Walter Raleigh from Richard Hakluyt discussing further settlement, he states a distinct preference for the Chesapeake Bay's bountiful land and water (quoted from *The Roanoke Voyages 1584-1590*, edited by David Beers Quinn).

Yf you proceed, which I longe much to know, in your enterprise of Virginia, your best planting will be aboute the bay of the Chesepians, to which latitude Peter Martyr and franciscus lopez de Gomara the Spaniard confesse that our Gabot and the English did first discover: which the Spaniardes here after cannot deny vu whensoever wee shall be at Peace with them.

So it was on the morning of April 26, 1607, that the three small ships named *Godspeed, Susan Constant* and *Discovery* made their way across the Atlantic Ocean and approached the sand dunes of present-day Virginia Beach. It would be

Replica of the Godspeed   *lg*

these settlers who would go on to establish the English settlement at Jamestown. But, they stopped here first, on Cape Henry, the tip of Virginia Beach where the Atlantic Ocean meets the Chesapeake Bay. The small fleet of three ships under the command of Christopher Newport sailed into the mouth of the Chesapeake Bay and anchored off the cape that they would name for their King James' elder son, Henry, Prince of Wales. The opposite shore to the east would be called Charles in honor of James' younger son. Later, it was James' daughter, Elizabeth, for whom the Elizabeth River in Norfolk was to be named. Not to omit the father, the settlers named the great river which fed into the Chesapeake the James River. Their first settlement, Jamestown, was also named in honor of the King of England.

On April 27, 1607 the crew of the expedition put together the shallop which they brought over in pieces. This boat could be rowed, sailed, paddled or poled. On April 28, 1607, it is recorded by George Percy that they visited a river on the southside which may have been the Lynnhaven River (quoted from http://etext.lib.virginia.edu/etcbin/jamestown-browse?id=J1002).

The seven and twentieth day we began to build up our Shallop: the Gentlemen and Souldiers marched eight miles up into the Land, we could not see a Savage in all that march, we came to a place where they had made a great fire, and had beene newly rosting Oysters: when they perceived our comming, they fled away to the Mountaines, and left many of the Oysters in the fire: we ate some of the Oysters, which were very large and delicate in taste.

The eighteenth [28th] day we launched our Shallop, the Captaine and some Gentlemen went in her, and discovered up the Bay, we found a River on the Southside running into the Maine; we entered it and found it very shoald water, not for any Boats to swim: wee went further into the Bay, and saw a plaine plot of ground where we went on Land, and found the place five mile in compasse, without either Bush or Tree, we saw nothing there but a Cannow, which was made out of the whole tree, which was five and forty foot long by the Rule. Upon this plot of ground we got good store of Mussels and Oysters, which lay on the ground as thicke as stones: wee opened some, and found in many of them Pearles. Wee marched some three or foure miles further into the Woods, where we saw great smoakes of fire. Wee marched to those smoakes and found that the Savages had beene there burning downe the grasse, as wee thought either to make their plantation there, or else to give signes to bring their forces together, and so to give us battell. We past through excellent ground full of Flowers of divers kinds and colours, and as goodly trees as I have seene, as Cedar, Cipresse, and other kindes: going a little further we came into a little plat of ground full of fine and beautifull Strawberries, foure times bigger and better than ours in England.

After a look around the local waters, on April 29, 1607 the sailors returned to Cape Henry, a landing party went ashore, and a cross was planted whereby the men claimed this land for God and England. It was thus that Virginia Beach, Virginia holds a unique place in history as this small group of the first permanent English settlers claimed our land in the name of James I, King of England.

Just 83 years later, in 1691, the villages that became Virginia Beach were referred to as Princess Anne County, which was formed from Lower Norfolk

Cross at Cape Henry   *vs*

County. The area was not to be called Virginia Beach until almost 200 years later. The earliest reference to the area as Virginia Beach is the name given to a club of hunters and fishermen who began a lodge in 1880 at the area near what is now 17th Street.

Old Princess Anne Hotel   *Collection of Lillie Gilbert*

When the railroad built a large resort near the eastern end of the rail line from Norfolk, the area called Virginia Beach was secured as a place name on maps. They called the 1884 hotel they built, Virginia Beach Hotel. After a few years, in 1888, renovated and additions made, the hotel reopened with its new name, Princess Anne. This four story seaside resort hotel marks the beginning of the present resort area. Notable for many amenities, it had over 300 electric light bulbs in 1888, and its own electric plant powered by an eighty horsepower engine (Mansfield, 1989). The hotel literally put Virginia Beach on the map even though all of the original Virginia Beach was but a tiny resort oceanfront community.

The area incorporated as a town in 1906 but was sparsely populated populated and extended northward from Rudee Inlet to approximately what is today Laskin Road/31st Street. The rest of the area was still Princess Anne County. Except for the lighthouse keepers and staff housing at Cape Henry, the last house along the oceanfront area in 1908 was the John M. Masury home. His was the only dwelling between 31st Street and Cape Henry, but this house wasn't even on the ocean. Dr. Masury built his 25 room stone mansion fronting Crystal Lake although he owned 130 acres of land with 800 yards overlooking the Atlantic. For paddlers on Crystal Lake, a look at this grand house makes for an interesting trip. See page 161.

Virginia Beach slowly grew and became an independent city in 1952 1952 that extended the boundaries from Rudee Inlet to 49th Street. In 1963, a merger with Princess Anne County formed the current 248 square mile city. Virginia Beach is the most populous city in the state and with over 440,000 residents is the 40th largest city in the United States.

Saving Ships and Lives

As a measure to save valuable cargo and reduce the loss of lives from ship-wrecks, in 1792, the first Cape Henry Lighthouse was completed. To supple-ment the safety of ships, the USLSS (U.S. Life-Saving Service) began in 1871.

The Cape Henry USLSS crew launching the surfboat

Photo courtesy Old Coast Guard collection

Cape Henry, Dam Neck Mills and False Cape were the first life-saving stations built in Virginia in 1874. Then Congress allotted more funds and Seatack and Little Island were added in 1878. On schedule, the patrols would depart and walk until they met the patrols coming from the adjoining stations. They would then exchange a metal check to show they had completed their patrol and return to their station (Pouliot & Pouliot, 1986).

Life-Saving Station False Cape

Collection of False Cape State Park

The Seatack station and Seatack area of Virginia Beach reportedly were named during the 1812 war when the British landed troops on the beach and attempted to make their way inland. Thus "sea attack" may have become "Seatack." This is a little hard to believe since there were so few dwellings and so few inhabitants to even witness an invasion. A more plausible explanation, perhaps, is that the name formed because sailing ships at sea sometimes had to tack (turn in order to achieve a desired final destination, originally to catch favored winds) away from the shore before the advent of the lighthouse system along the Atlantic Coast in order to make the moves necessary to avoid shoals along the beachfront. The last "tack to seaward" or sea tack approaching Cape Henry from the south may also account for the name. Today, looking out to sea, the viewer can spot the Chesapeake Light, which is the safe tack or turning area for ships headed out to sea or into the entrance for the Chesapeake Bay.

Only two existing buildings of the life-saving stations remain in Virginia Beach: the Little Island Life-Saving Station at Sandbridge Beach in the southeastern part of Virginia Beach and the Old Coast Guard Station at 24th Street in Virginia Breach along the resort strip. The original 1878 Little Island Station buildings were lost in the hurricane of August 23,

1933. The building now used as Little Island Park office is the 1925 station which was turned over to the GSA in 1964 and made a city park two years later.

Seatack Life-Saving Station   *Collection of Old Coast Guard Station*

The Seatack Life-Saving Station is now known as the Old Coast Guard Station and is a museum and gift shop. This facility was built in 1903 and has been turned 90 degrees from its original position in the 24th Street Park, adjacent to the site. The original station, which was built in 1878, was located across Atlantic Avenue where the post office is now located. The Virginia Beach Station was decommissioned in 1969. The U.S. Life- Saving Service and the Revenue Cutter Service merged and the combined service was named the U.S. Coast Guard in 1915.

Historic Storm and Shipwreck

During a violent storm on April 7, 1889, more than two hundred ships wrecked between Cape Hatteras and Cape Henry. The *Benjamin F. Poole* was bound for Baltimore to pick up a load of coal and was riding high in the water. As the crew battled the storm, the captain realized the ship would never make the safe anchorage of Lynnhaven Roads or Hampton Roads. As a last-ditch effort, he decided to beach the schooner. It came to rest in front of the fashionable Princess Anne Hotel. The Seatack Life-Saving Service brought all of the crew to shore with the aid of a breeches buoy. As soon as the storm subsided, plans for rescuing the ship began. Several attempts were made to refloat the vessel and finally to protect it, sheet piling was put into the sand around the boat, forming a sort of dry dock. An offshore anchor and buoy was connected to the ship by a ten inch hawser of rope. For seventeen months, Captain Hjalmar Charlton lived aboard the ship to protect it from salvagers. It stayed put as no high tide was large enough to float it. Finally during a three day nor'easter in September of 1890, the salvage crew with their rescue tug was able to pull up the anchor and heave on the large rope and tow the schooner to port for repairs. During the Poole's "residence" on the shoreline, very few guests at the hotel knew that the beach curiosity they were able to visit housed a honeymoon couple during its last three months (Wichard, 1959). In 1956, the bride, Matilda Charlton tells the following story to a local newspaper (Kyle, 1956).

Gladly will I go back sixty years and tell you what I remember of Virginia Beach in 1890. It consisted of fourteen cottages and two hotels, the Princess Anne, and the Ocean View (**Author's Note:** The hotel was the Ocean Sands Hotel). *There was a foot boardwalk from the Princess Anne and a very sandy walk of about a hundreds feet to the vessel in which I lived for three months. The vessel was a very large and beautiful four-masted schooner, and during that summer we had many visitors come aboard.*

I remember vividly my experience when the northeaster began on September 28, 1890 and continued until October 3rd. My husband, the ship's captain, thinking I would be safer off the ship, wrapped me in oil skins and he and the pilot, Captain Cunningham from Norfolk, attempted to escort me from the ship. The wind was howling and the beach had been cut away at least four feet high. Between the two men I was finally landed at the Seatack Life-Saving Station, where I spent the night.

I could hear the roar of the breakers and knowing my husband was aboard the ship I was almost frantic. To make matters worse, Captain Drinkwater of the Life-Saving Station said, "She will break up and I will use her cabin panels for a new home." However, the vessel weathered the gale and I withstood the night.

The vessel had moved fifty feet and as the storm continued, I was again wrapped in oil skins and escorted to Norfolk, where I continued my journey to my home in Baltimore.

I never thought then that Virginia Beach would ever be the resort it is now.

Early Ecotourism

Before the city of Virginia Beach existed, or the first hotel built, the area around Cape Henry was a popular visitation spot. Because there were few, if any, beachfront inhabitants and no roads, visitation was by boat. Steamers from Norfolk provided a way to see the wild coast. (See ad below.)

PLEASURE EXCURSION TO THE CAPES

The elegant steam boat Norfolk, (of the Commercial Line,) Capt. Weems, will leave Norfolk on Saturday, the 7th July, at 8 o'clock in the morning, for Cape Henry – touching at Portsmouth and Old Point Comfort, and return to Norfolk by sun set.   Passage and Dinner, $2.

July 3, 1827, *The American Beacon* newspaper, Norfolk

Historic Landmarks at the Beach

From a paddler's perspective, the older landmarks seen from the water are all too well blended with the new skyline to be able to pick them out. Jumping back over a hundred years, almost all of the Beach's landmarks were centered at the oceanfront. From the North Carolina line and traveling north into Virginia, the old seafarers would have seen the False Cape Life-Saving Station and a few houses, then the same view repeated at Little Island, then again at Dam Neck. Here at Dam Neck, the water traveler would have seen the windmills. The area was formerly called Dam Neck Mills. Today the beachfront houses the Dam Neck Fleet Combat Training Center, Atlantic and 12 tenant commands. The Seatack Life-Saving Station would be next along with several beachfront houses by the 1920s. In 1927 the Cavalier Hotel became the tallest structure along the beach. At the Atlantic beach's north end stand the two Cape Henry lighthouses, one from 1792 and the other, 1881.

The Hunt Room at the Old Cavalier Hotel

Originally a private club, the Hunt Room was exclusively the domain of the gentlemen who visited the Cavalier and hunted or fished at the spacious resort. Any game or fish that were captured on the grounds of the hotel, including the oceanfront, were prepared by the kitchen staff and served. Wealthy horsemen, hunters and sportsmen enjoyed a small pub and dining area. Walking into the warm room on a cold winter's evening, during the Jazz Age of the 1920s and 30s, one might see notables such as F. Scott Fitzgerald, Will Rogers, or Fatty Arbuckle. Many other celebrities were warmed by a fire in the old hearth at the Hunt Room. No fewer than seven Presidents have stayed at the Cavalier Hotel. Richard Nixon may have visited the Hunt Room when his daughter, Julie, lived for a short time in an oceanfront home near 56th Street in the early 1970's.

Closed for a long time, the Hunt Room reopened for January, February, and March beginning in 1993. No longer the haunt of the male only crowd, today's cozy Hunt Room invites all. Complete with comfortable sofas and a huge fireplace, the place has a snow country feel, like a ski lodge or an old friend's den. The fireplace is the centerpiece of the Hunt Room with a commanding presence of 8 feet long, 5 feet deep and 5 feet high (Parker, 2003). Plan to have dinner here if possible. For more information, call 757-425-8555.

Atlantic Wildfowl Heritage Museum and the Back Bay Wildfowl Guild, Inc.

Named for the last private owners of this beautiful old beach house, the DeWitt cottage was built in 1895 by Bernard P. Holland. After the Hollands moved a block off the waterfront, the property was purchased in 1909 by Cornelius DeWitt. It remained in the DeWitt family until 1988. Built to last, the house has fourteen-inch brick walls, allowing it to be cool in the warmer months. It was heated by fireplaces. Typical of larger cottages built at the time, it has twenty-two rooms, a basement and an attic. The cottage is now home to the Atlantic Wildfowl Heritage Museum and the Back Bay Wildfowl Guild, Inc. (a nonprofit organization) and is listed on the Virginia Landmarks Register. The cottage is located at 1113 Atlantic Avenue, Virginia Beach, VA 23451, 757-437-8432 – City of Virginia Beach, owner. For more information visit www.awhm.org.

Horses in the City

Wild horses may have walked the beaches of North Carolina and Virginia for hundreds of years. Our early settlers and Life-Saving crews used horses regularly, and during the 1930s, the Cavalier Hotel provided horseback riding along dune and forest trails to adventuresome guests.

In Virginia Beach today, the only horses allowed along the beachfront belong to the men in blue or by special city permit. The horses and riders seen along the resort strip are part of the Virginia Beach Police Mounted Patrol, members of the Second Police Precinct. This helpful patrol got its start locally in 1985. During the summer months the unit patrols the resort area and at other times of the year works various locations and special events. Major advantages of being on horseback are the ability to go into areas not easily accessible to vehicles and to see from a high vantage point as well as to be seen. The mounted patrol is popular with residents and visitors and is seen as a very successful public relations effort.

In November, 2001, the patrol got a permanent home and the facility was dedicated in March of 2002. The address is 2089 Indian River Road in Virginia Beach, near the Pungo intersection. This horse farm consists of about 40 acres with 20 acres being pasture. There are plans to host competitions and clinics for other horse patrol units in the indoor and outdoor rings and 10,000 square foot arena. There are currently two barns and storage areas. For the two-footed team members the amenities include office space, meeting rooms, and storage. Training for the Patrol is a 10-week period and an officer must have completed at least three years on the streets before being considered for the equine post (Evans-Hylton, 2002). Their season at the Oceanfront begins May 1 of each year and extends through the summer months.

Cape Henry

Cape Henry houses Fort Story, an army base. The 1,451-acre base with 3.6 miles of waterfront was established in 1914 and named for Virginia-born artillery expert Brigadier General John Patten Story. Aside from the U.S. Army base, the broad cape also houses civilians in modest to glorious homes and a Virginia State Park, First Landing, renamed from its original title of Seashore State Park.

The Cape Henry Lighthouses

Save some time to drive to and explore the original Cape Henry Lighthouse dating from 1792. Soon after the settlers landed at Cape Henry, the need for a beacon became apparent. Many of the settlers took up farming and relied on ships to transport their products to distant ports. Initially they would use bonfires on the beach to aid navigators. Entrance into the Chesapeake Bay was a hazardous task, causing the early colonists to request a beacon from the governing council. But it wasn't until 1773 that materials were delivered, but construction of the lighthouse was brought to a halt by the Revolutionary War. Finally after the war, funds were appropriated for the lighthouse by President George Washington and it was completed in late October 1792. It is the first public works project that was authorized by the United States Congress.

The original lighthouse is an octagonal structure built on the tallest sand dune at Cape Henry. The sandstone used to build it is the same that was used at Mt. Vernon, the Capitol and the White House, all quarried in Aquia and Rappahannock, Virginia. The lighting apparatus was damaged during the Civil war, making entry into the Chesapeake Bay difficult for navigation. The original Fresnel lens made in France was removed in 1881 and its location remains a mystery to this day. This original Cape Henry Lighthouse is owned and maintained by the Association for the Preservation of Virginia Anti-quities (APVA). The Old Cape Henry

The newer Cape Henry Lighthouse   *vs*

Lighthouse is listed as a National Historic Engineering Landmark by the American Society of Civil Engineers and also on the National Register of Historic Landmarks.

The old lighthouse can be climbed for a small admission fee and is open year-round. The 360-degree view is worth the effort if one has no fear of heights or tight places. Seeing juvenile humpback whales or Atlantic bottle-nosed dolphins might reward the viewer, depending on the time of year. On a clear day, the eastern shore of Virginia is easily seen. Do take binoculars.

There are now two Cape Henry Lighthouses, the newer one located less than 400 feet from the original. The second was completed in 1881 and is made of 1,700,000 ponds of cast iron. At 163 feet, it is the tallest fully enclosed cast iron lighthouse in the U.S. and is fully operational. While the Old Cape Henry Light was lit by whale oil, the newer Lighthouse is now powered by electricity with a back-up generator. Both lighthouses are located just a little north of the Atlantic Avenue entrance to Fort Story.

For more information or updates as to opening times or fees, contact the Old Cape Henry Lighthouse Visitor Center at 757-422-9421 or visit www.apva.org. the Old Cape Henry Lighthouse Visitor Center at 757-422-9421.

In the absence of a lighthouse (before 1792), the mariner dared to stand (hold course) into the Bay regardless of the hour and visibility only if he were experienced in sailing those waters and certain of his latitude. More commonly mariners did not do so unless there remained enough hours of daylight to clear the capes and come to anchor in Lynnhaven Roads before dark.

Arthur Pierce Middleton, *Tobacco Coast*

Part 5

Lynnhaven River and its tributaries

Lynnhaven River and its tributaries

Lynnhaven Bay is a portion of the Chesapeake, at its southern extremity, and lies between Cape Henry and a point at Little Creek Inlet. The waters of the Chesapeake here make a graceful curve into the land; and the view, to the north especially, is extensive, and very beautiful. Lynnhaven River is, also, a truly beautiful collection of water, which extends into Princess Anne County from the bay.

-William S. Forrest, 1853

A tidal tributary to the southern end of the Chesapeake Bay, the "collection of water" that comprises the historic Lynnhaven River, not including Lynnhaven Bay, is usually referred to as the Eastern and Western Branch, but there are many small creeks and bays which make up the entire watershed. Lynnhaven Bay is formed by the Eastern and Western Branches of the Lynnhaven River, which empty into it. From Lynnhaven Bay through Long Creek's two channels, the waters of Broad Bay and Linkhorn Bay along with their tributaries help comprise the eastern most part of the watershed.

Location

The Lynnhaven River's watershed is basically bounded on the east by the Atlantic Ocean, Kempsville to the south, Independence Boulevard to the west and the Chesapeake Bay to the north.

Access Points

EASTERN BRANCH OF THE LYNNHAVEN RIVER
A. Lynnhaven Inlet
B. Hutton Lane
C. Lynnhaven Parkway South

LONG CREEK/BROAD BAY/ LINKHORN BAY
A. 64th Street at First Landing State Park

WESTERN BRANCH OF THE LYNNHAVEN RIVER
A. Lynnhaven Inlet

The Lynnhaven watershed covers 64 square miles representing one-fifth of the land mass and is home to about 200,000 people, roughly half of the population of Virginia Beach. The diagrams on the next 2 pages outline the tributaries of the Eastern and Western Branches as well as Long Creek and associated waterways. Not outlined are Dix Creek and Keeling Cove which are in Lynnhaven Bay proper or Lake Joyce which was formerly navigable to Lynnhaven Bay via Pleasure House Creek.

Paddling Tip:

The Lynnhaven is a shallow bay and it may be wise to follow channel markers or crab pot buoys at lower tide levels.

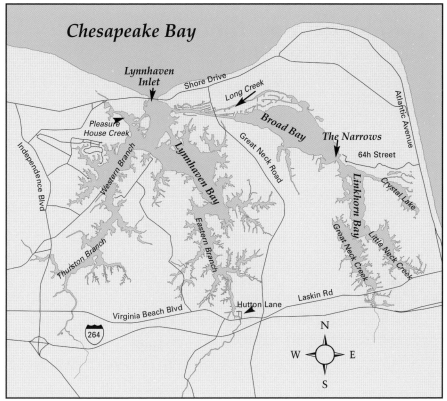

Map 24: Lynnhaven River & its tributaries

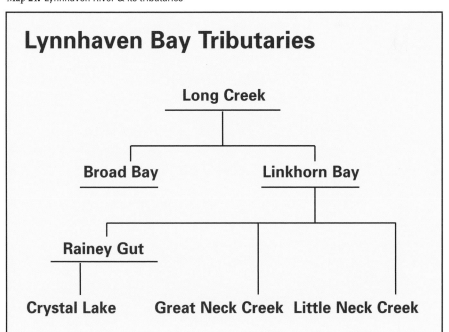

Lynnhaven Bay Tributaries

Long Creek

Broad Bay   Linkhorn Bay

Rainey Gut

Crystal Lake   Great Neck Creek   Little Neck Creek

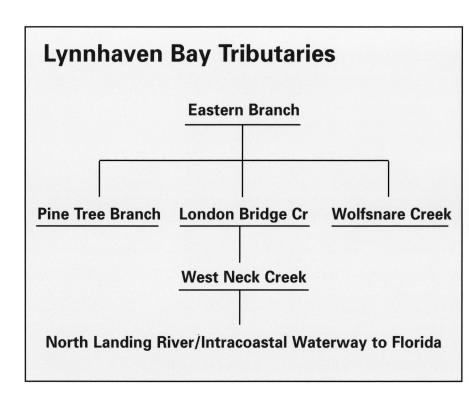

Lynnhaven Bay Tributaries

Eastern Branch

Pine Tree Branch   London Bridge Cr   Wolfsnare Creek

West Neck Creek

North Landing River/Intracoastal Waterway to Florida

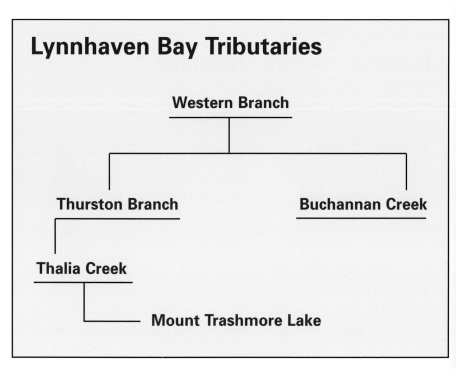

Lynnhaven Bay Tributaries

Western Branch

Thurston Branch   Buchannan Creek

Thalia Creek

Mount Trashmore Lake

History of the Lynnhaven

The Lynnhaven River's name at the time of settlement around twenty years after Jamestown was "Chesopean River." The earliest mention of the "Lyn Haven" that these authors have found is on a 1634 grant to Henry Southell who received 700 acres "upon the Chesopean shore, within the Territory of Lyn Haven" (Nugent, 1992).

It is widely believed that colonist Adam Thoroughgood named the Lynnhaven River for the land of Kings Lin near his birthplace in England. When Captain Adam Thoroughgood transported 105 people in several different ships from 1628 to 1634, he was awarded 50 acres for each soul plus "50 acres for his per adv. [personal adventure], 50 ac. for per adv. of his wife Sarah Thoroughgood" (Nugent, 1992). The 5350 acres he was granted were bordered to the north by the Chesapeake Bay and east by "the first CR. of that river" which would have been the Lynnhaven, westerly "into the maine land" and southerly to an unnamed island in the river. With this land and 200 acres purchased in 1634 and 600 acres granted in 1637 (Nugent, 1992), Thoroughgood became the largest landholder on "Lyn haven alias the Chesopean Riv."

The land in the northern portion of what is now Virginia Beach was known as Linhaven Parish of Lower Norfolk when Elizabeth City County was divided in 1638. An early rendering of the "Lin haven" River is on a 1651 map of Virginia Farrer. Her father, John Farrer, was an investor in the Virginia Company and named his daughter "so that speaking unto her, looking upon her, and hearing others call her by name, he might think upon both at once" (Fischer and Kelly, 2000). The Virginia Company of London had been given a royal charter to colonize anywhere between the 34th and 45th parallels. The huge territory of Virginia was therefore considered to be all the land north of today's Cape Hatteras and the Canadian border. Farrer's 1651 map is interesting not only because it names the "Lin haven" but that it places the Sea of China and the Indies just behind what we know as the Blue Ridge Mountains.

Ten years before the Farrer map, Sir William Berkeley sailed to this New World and brought with him the king's commission as a governor of Virginia, an office he held on and off for thirty-five years. He was surprised to find that the colony consisted of "8,000 sickly souls," but by the end of Berkeley's tenure in 1677 Virginia's population had risen to 40,000 (Fischer and Kelly, 2000).

In the early years of the settlement along the Lynnhaven River all court proceedings took place at the church with the vestry as jurors. It was the mandate of the Crown that the Virginia Colony set up churches and courthouses close to each other and the population base. In 1661 the first courthouse in Lower Norfolk County was built at Broad Creek. With the population spreading, in 1689 two courthouses replaced the first one, always close to water as the rivers were the easiest travel routes before passable roads were built and maintained. These new courthouses were on the Elizabeth River and Wolfsnare Creek off the Eastern Branch of the Lynnhaven River.

Historic Homes along the Lynnhaven Watershed

Almost all of the early structures have been lost to shoreline erosion or decay over the centuries. There are still some early homes that have been restored and are open for viewing. Notable among these, but not visible from the water, are the Francis Land House (ca.1805-1810), Lynnhaven House (ca.1725), Thoroughgood House (ca.1680) and Upper Wolfsnare (ca.1759). The Walke Manor House, built by William Walke in 1751 burned in 1828. The good bricks from the ruins were retrieved and used to build Ferry Plantation House which was completed circa 1830. This house is at Ferry Point at the southern end of the Western Branch of the Lynnhaven.

A waterfront home that still remains as a private residence is the Adam Keeling house. Recent dendrochronology work indicates the house timbers to have been felled in 1734/35 (Miles and Worthington, 2006). Called "Ye Dudlies," this is one of the oldest houses in Virginia Beach and thought to be built by a descendant of Adam Keeling (1639-1683), son of an early settler, Thomas Keeling, who received a land grant in 1635 in the area known as Great Neck Point. It is interesting to note that it was Adam Thoroughgood who transported Thomas Keeling to Virginia aboard the *Hopewell* in 1628 (Nugent, 1992). Thomas later named two sons Adam and Thorowgood. Adam Thoroughgood was the godfather of Adam Keeling and in his will left Adam Keeling a breeding goat (Maling, 1992). The Keeling house has beautiful patterned brickwork of glazed headers on the north side. It can be glimpsed from Adam Keeling Road, but please be aware that this is a private home and do not intrude on the current owners.

Lynnhaven Roads

Because movement by water was far easier than on land, early settlers centered their houses and farms close to the water. The early colonial roadways on land were probably built on old animal trails or American Indian trails. The terms "road or roads" were a safe anchorage, often a convergence of waterways. In *The Encyclopedia of Nautical Knowledge*, the definition reads, "ROAD. Also roads; roadstead; an anchorage, a large partly protected area in which vessels may anchor. Open r., usually open roadstead, such area protected from gales by near-by land only" (McEwen and Lewis, 1953). The "roads" of Hampton Roads referred not to highways on land but the safe anchorage and place where several rivers joined waters of the lower Chesapeake. On a 1781 French map of this area, "Rade D'Hampton" is clearly shown as the waterway between present-day Hampton and Willoughby. Lynnhaven Roads was and is the area just north of the mouth of Lynnhaven Inlet. Boats have traditionally used this area as a slightly sheltered harbor from currents that run north/south along the Chesapeake coastline to Cape Henry. A few of the

1607 Re-enactment at First Landing State Park   *lg*

sailing ships involved with OpSail 2000 anchored here during the maritime gathering to celebrate the new millennium. Witnessing the three-masted schooners and other tall ships anchored in the Bay and in Lynnhaven Roads was like a step back in time when sailing ships plied these waters. It may have been in Lynnhaven Roads that the three small ships that brought the first permanent English settlers to The New World sought safe harbor for the few days that they spent here in 1607.

Eastern Branch of the Lynnhaven River

The Eastern Branch is approximately 6 miles in length and covers approximately 1,900 acres. The depth of the river varies widely from 2-10 feet at mean low water to 6-12 feet (MLW) in the dredged channels.

Most of this wider side of the Lynnhaven looks a lot like the Western Branch: tidal estuary with salt marshes. Many large homes dot the shoreline. Typically, the virtual lines formed by crab pots mark areas deep enough for canoes and kayaks at low tide while some coves become unpaddleable. Ospreys are a common sight and build their nests on tops of pilings or platforms bordering the waterway.

Osprey nest on platform in Lynnhaven River   *vs*

Winds and Tides in the Lynnhaven

Lunar tides affect the watershed as far as the beginnings of West Neck Creek to the south. The mean lunar tide ranges from 0.8 to 2 feet depending on location and may surge higher depending on the winds. Typically, strong easterly or northerly winds raise normal tidal levels and may cause coastal flooding. During periods of strong winds, the shallow waters of Lynnhaven Bay, Broad Bay and Linkhorn Bay can be quite rough for small craft such as kayaks and canoes. Paddlers are advised to check weather and tidal conditions when planning a day on the Lynnhaven and its tributaries.

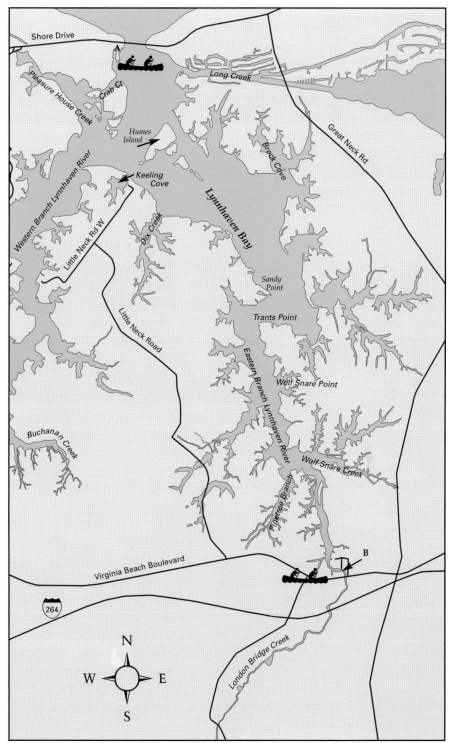

Map 25: Eastern Branch of the Lynnhaven River

© *Vickie Shufer*

Access Points

A. Lynnhaven Inlet at Crab Creek

Directions: From U.S. Route 60/Shore Drive, the Lynnhaven Boat and Beach Facility is located at the southwest side of the Lesner Bridge on U.S. Route 60/Shore Drive and is accessible to motorized and non-motorized boat traffic. The kayak launch area is a small sandy beach just to the right as one enters the parking lot. There is a small fee to park. There are many amenities at this access site. For additional information, contact the Virginia Beach Department of Parks and Recreation at 757-385-4461.

Facilities: Vending machines and an information booth are on site as are restrooms, drinking water and an outdoor shower. There are no picnic tables, but several restaurants are close by. Swimming is not allowed because the concrete ramps serve as a launch site for motor boats and personal watercraft. This facility is open 24 hours a day.

Portage lane to the access dock.   *lg*

B. Hutton Lane

Directions: Look for the Hutton Lane access near Pep Boys' Automotive Center on the northeast side of the river. Another landmark is Dunkin Donuts at 2448 Virginia Beach Boulevard. The access parking is actually off of Hutton Circle but is referred to as the Hutton Lane access since a street sign for Hutton Lane is visible from Virginia Beach Boulevard. To get to the access, drive north on Hutton Lane beside Pep Boys' parking lot. Hutton Lane quickly comes to a dead end. Turn to the west (left), and then turn south (left) on Hutton Circle. It's a short drive to the end of the cul-de-sac. Be careful

Hutton Lane walkway   *lg*

not to park on private property or block the neighbors. There is parking for a few cars. Look for the asphalt path leading to the river. The floating dock is designed as a launch for kayak and canoes. London Bridge Creek begins here and leads south. By heading north, the paddler is at the beginning of the Eastern Branch of the Lynnhaven River.

Access site at Hutton Lane   *vs*   Lynnhaven Parkway north   *lg*

C. Lynnhaven Parkway South

Directions: Go south on Lynnhaven Parkway from Virginia Beach Boulevard approximately 1⁷⁄₁₀ miles. There is a small shopping center on the southeast side of Lynnhaven Parkway with limited parking. Ask permission from the store owners to park and launch here.

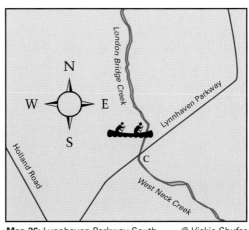

Map 26: Lynnhaven Parkway South   *© Vickie Shufer*

Paddling Sections

THE EASTERN BRANCH OF THE LYNNHAVEN RIVER

1. **(A) Crab Creek to (B) Hutton Lane, 7⅓ miles**
2. **(B) Hutton Lane to (C) Lynnhaven Parkway South, 3½ miles**

Section 1. (A) Crab Creek to (B) Hutton Lane, 7⅓ mile

From Crab Creek, a paddler has a number of paddling options, depending on how far one wants to paddle and the paddling conditions. The water level is influenced by the lunar tides, with two low tides and two high tides each day. At low tide some of the smaller creeks and tributaries may be too shallow for paddling, so the paddler may choose to paddle some of the larger, deeper waterways. Along this route, many large waterfront homes will be seen. Imagine how this area might have looked in colonial times or to the first inhabitants, the Chesapean Indians. There are no take-out points along the way. Almost all of the land is privately owned. The various small coves and waterways and even today's subdivision names have historical connections.

To reach Hutton Lane, paddle south/southeast to Lynnhaven Bay around Humes Island. Great Neck peninsula will be on the east and Little Neck peninsula on the west. This portion of the route is along the Eastern Branch of the Lynnhaven River. Trants Point is 3½ miles south of Crab Creek. Continue south approximately 1½ miles to Wolf Snare Point. From Wolf Snare Point the paddler may decide to travel into Pinetree Branch, which looks like the correct way to paddle. It's a straight route and not immediately clear that it narrows quickly. Pinetree Branch used to be the waterway that led to the Francis Land House. Largely filled in by sediment and downfall, this old waterway south of Virginia Beach Boulevard is still visible through the marsh and can be paddled only at very high water. Paddling from Wolf Snare Point and following the main channel to the east, be sure to take the southerly turn. Other-wise the paddler will be in Wolf Snare Creek which doesn't go far. Soon the paddler will be at the Hutton Lane access site.

Paddler on Crab Creek   vs

144

Francis Land House

The Francis Land House is a 200 year old plantation home built circa 1805-1810. It is located at 3131 Virginia Beach Boulevard and is open to the public for guided tours. A boardwalk trail winds through a small forest to the marsh. There you can read about the early life in what was to be Virginia Beach and about the large canoes or lighters that carried goods to waiting vessels in the Lynnhaven. For more information, call 757-385-5100.

River Highlights

The natural features bordering the Lynnhaven include mostly saltmarsh habitats. Native plants that grow here have adapted to the saltmarsh environment in a number of ways. Saltmarsh cordgrass forms colonies at the edge of the low tide zone. They have adapted by excreting salt on their surface. To test the saltiness of the water, hold a blade of grass between two fingers and pull it through them. You can feel the salt on your fingers.

Great egrets, great blue herons, osprey, kingfishers are among the fish-eating birds seen on the waterway. Mallards are permanent residents and in the spring can be seen with their young trailing behind them.

Saltmarsh cordgrass community along Crab Creek   *vs*

Historical Sites

Eastern Shore Chapel

In 1640, the colonial English residents of Lynnhaven Parish attended church services at a building constructed on the Western Branch of the Lynnhaven River. In 1649, there were only 20 churches in all of Virginia to serve a total population of around 15,000 English settlers (Nugent, 1992).

By the 1680s, the residents of this area had grown in number and now lived on both sides of the Lynnhaven River: the Eastern Branch and the Western Branch. Given that roads were few and the trip by foot, boat, horseback, or wagon involved much time and labor to accomplish, the residents on the eastern shore of the Lynnhaven River requested that a second church be built for that growing sector of the community. The name Eastern Shore Chapel aptly described its location, as it was on the eastern shore of the Lynnhaven. "Wolf's Snare Creek" was chosen for the first location for the church because of its landing, already conveniently established for trade and commerce.

In 1724 a new chapel was built, not far from the older creekside location. The land was provided by the Cornick family whose land holdings they referred to as Salisbury Plains. The land patent of 500 acres had been given to William Cornix in 1657 and it was he who coined the name, "Salsbury Plaines" (Nugent, 1992). The large, brick plantation house, no longer standing, was not completed until 1727, exactly 27 years after William's death. Not surprisingly, the home was called Salisbury Plains.

By 1754 a third church was constructed next to the older one. This structure served the community for almost 200 years. The name Salisbury Plains was still in use into the 1930s to describe the area and the old home. Eventually, the construction of part of the Oceana Naval Air Station caused the church to be relocated. And move it, the congregation did! They managed to salvage some useable bricks, the stained glass windows, pews, ceremonial crosses, baptismal font, and the original silver communion set. The most difficult task was the relocation of the cemetery graves. The current church (and its cemetery) is located on 20 acres of land at 2020 Laskin Road in Virginia Beach.

Shorehaven

Bordering Lynnhaven Bay and adjacent to Great Neck Park is the neighborhood that shares its name with the dog-leg street that leads to it from Great Neck Road. This neighborhood in Great Neck was named after the Shorehaven farmhouse that was over 100 years old before its demise sometime after 1987. The area was developed by the Braggs beginning in 1970). Avery Island, today not an island, is Shorehaven's southernmost point of land. Recalled a neighbor who grew up on Back Cove Road, a group of oystermen used to have a small bridge that connected the neighborhood to what is today called Rose Hall Shores. Holly Point Road is the current name for the place where bridge met old roadway.

Inlynnview

R.F. Trant in the 1930s owned the land on which this neighborhood was built. His large, two-story shingle home was called Inlynnview Hall ("In" for Indian grounds, "Lynn" for Lynnhaven River, and "view" for the lovely terrain), for which Inlynnview Road, the main street of the neighborhood, gets its name (hamptonroads.com).

Wolf Snare

This area's two historic manor houses, Upper and Lower Wolfsnare, were named after the "Wolfe Snare" Creek that meanders west across the lower end of present day Great Neck and enters the Eastern Branch of the Lynnhaven River just north of London Bridge. This creek is named in historic records of the area dating as far back the 1600s. An explanation of the name is from Walke Family Scrapbook (Tazewell, 1982).

"The earliest settlers of this part of Virginia had Indians as well as packs of wolves to endanger their lives. The wolves also killed precious livestock brought over from England. To snare a wolf deep pits were dug, covered with twigs and branches and leaves. The traps were baited and the weight of the wolf caused him to fall into the pit and be captured. A bounty was given for all wolves killed. Long after there was no danger from wolves in the area of Wolf Snare Creek, the deep pits remained and were seen as late as the beginning of this [20th] century."

As testament to the wolves' numbers and the threat they posed, by the mid 1600s the bounty offered for killing one had been raised from 50 to 200 pounds of tobacco (Turner, 1984).

Rivers must have been the guides which conducted the footsteps of the first travelers. They are the constant lure, when they flow by our doors, to distant enterprise and adventure…   Henry David Thoreau

Upper Wolfsnare Plantation House

Near Wolf Snare Point is the Upper Wolfsnare plantation home, built by Thomas Walke III and bequeathed to Thomas Walke IV. When the house was built circa 1759, nearby Wolf Snare Creek was navigable and small craft could get near the house to load or unload supplies. Today the only way to get to the house is to drive to 2040 Potter's Road. It is open to the public from Noon - 4:00 p.m. on Wednesday during July and August or by group appointment. For more information contact the Princess Anne/Virginia Beach Historical Society, the current owners at 757-491-3439 or www.virginiabeachhistory.org.

Near the same point of land was a trading post for the early settlers known as Pallett's Landing where it is said English ships would land (Kyle, 1969). This leads to a lot of speculation as to the size of the ships and the depth of the water. Smaller draft vessels called lighters were sent from the various landings of the settlers to the larger ships in the Lynnhaven to load or offload trade goods. It is at the head of Wolf Snare Creek that the first Eastern Shore (of the Lynnhaven) Chapel was built. The exact date is unknown, but is probably before 1660 since so many settlers were living on the east side of the Lynnhaven River around this time (Kyle, 1969).

Section 2. (B) Hutton Lane to (C) Lynnhaven Parkway South, 3½ miles

The trip on London Bridge Creek is an interesting paddle: urban, industrial and natural marsh. There is a treat awaiting the paddler with the willingness to paddle this section. After passing under Virginia Beach Boulevard and a railroad bridge, the waterway is more of a meandering marsh environment. Wading birds appear along with dabbling ducks. In recent years an otter family has been reported as well as nutria

A meandering tributary of London Bridge Creek   lg

148

and muskrats in view of office and residential buildings. Before passing under the Lynnhaven Parkway and just as the creek makes an abrupt turn west, look through the trees along the southern shore for a glimpse of Lower Wolfsnare House. This is a private house. Please do not intrude. This tributary of the Lynnhaven will pass under Lynnhaven Parkway North and shortly the creek becomes a manmade waterway.

After a lot of urban paddling and two more bridges, the take-out site is the bridge at Lynnhaven Parkway South. After this bridge, London Bridge Creek is called West Neck Creek. The water from this point south leads to the North Landing River and would eventually take the water traveler all the way to Florida via the Intracoastal Waterway! For information on West Neck Creek and the North Landing River, please refer to the authors' first book, *Wild River Guide to the North Landing River and Its Tributaries.*

Fiddlers

When approaching the mud flats, especially at low tide, the paddler may notice a flurry of activity amongst the cordgrasses as numerous crabs scurry to seek shelter in their burrows in the mud. These are the fiddler crabs, so named because of the large claw that the male crab waves in the air, either to attract attention or to intimidate a potential predator. Burrows are made by scraping up mud and forming it into pellets which are carried four or five feet away from the hole and then dropped. The process is repeated until the hole is deep enough (Perry, 1985).

vs

London Bridge Creek History

In the 18th century, the London Company of England built a trading post on a tributary of the eastern branch of the Lynnhaven River. Its wharf, built over what was to be called London Bridge Creek, was part of the well-used road that connected Kemps Landing (later, Kempsville) with the Eastern Shore Chapel (Jordan & Jordan, 1975). London Bridge is noted on the 1700s Benedict Arnold map.

Long Creek/Broad Bay/Linkhorn Bay

East of Lynnhaven Inlet, Long Creek's two channels are the connectors between the Lynnhaven and Broad Bay which leads to Linkhorn Bay. The Long Creek/Broad Bay/Linkhorn Bay water area is approximately 1,500 acres and is about 9 miles in length. The more northern of the two Long Creeks is the original creek. The other channel was dug during the 1930s. This has created more waterfront housing and marinas allowing more boats to pass along the waterway to and from the Lynnhaven.

Access Points
A. 64th Street at First Landing State Park

Directions: From U.S. Route 60/Shore Drive, head east to Atlantic Avenue and turn south. Shore Drive is also 83rd Street, so after making the turn on Atlantic, one only has to drive 19 blocks. If driving from I-264, go to the east end to Atlantic Avenue and turn north (left). Turn west on 64th Street and First Landing State Park's entrance is within a block. Pay the entrance fee and drive to the end of the road. Put in at the sandy beach at the end of this road. The park closes at dusk so plan paddling activities accordingly. This launch area is called The Narrows. Pictured below is a paved boat ramp at the end of the parking lot which can also be used for launching.

Facilities: The sandy beach is a good picnic spot with shady spots or sunny spots, however there are no picnic tables. Swimming is not allowed here. There are restroom facilities, vending machines and drinking water at the paved parking area. This part of the park closes at dusk.

Sandy beach at First Landing State Park

Collection of Lillie Gilbert

Rob Salway and Jason Andrews launch kayaks from the concrete boat ramp at The Narrows

vs

Mill Dam

There was a 1761 petition of William Godfrey, who held land on one side of the "Mill Dam Run," to build a water grist mill (Creecy, 1954). Today's Mill Dam Creek is impassable and is partially silted in, but the elevation of the land around it suggests that the mill (if it were near here) might have been a small tide mill.

Whether the area's tides could be harnessed to create enough power to turn a grist mill is open to speculation, but colonial tide mills were recorded on the Lynnhaven near Ferry Plantation and in Norfolk on the Eastern Branch of the Elizabeth River (on a creek also called Mill Dam Creek). In speaking of North Carolina's coastal region, it is written, "The incoming tides had been impounded to turn the wheels of sawmills and gristmills during the colonial period, and a statute of 1715 had authorized the condemnation of sites for 'publick mills.' In spite of the topography of the coastal plain, many waterpower mills were in existence" (Henderson, 1941). Early tide mills in England were found along shallow tidal creeks, several miles from the actual coast so as to be protected from ocean surges or troublesome waves, but still within the range of the tide. There were ponds behind the mills, formed by building a dike or dam landward of an estuary or creek that drained into a larger river or bay. At high tide, floodgates would be opened and water would enter the pond or retention area. The impounded water would be released at lower tide, turning the mill gears. Since so many of our early settlers here were from England, we can expect that they brought the knowledge of water mill or tide mill technology with them.

Early Land Roads along Lynnhaven's Eastern Branch

First Colonial Road's name derives from the first colonial church built on the eastern side of the Lynnhaven. Today's Mill Dam Road passes over an offshoot of Overstreet Cove which leads to Broad Bay. There is another old road of importance in this neighborhood: Great Neck Road. This too is along high ground, part of the Pungo Ridge, and passes by what in colonial times was referred to as Indian Fields. There are constant references to these fields as boundaries or locaters in the colonial record books. The places change but our roots to the colonial times are imbedded in the old names of our roadways and waterways.

Paddling Sections

LONG CREEK/BROAD BAY/LINKHORN BAY

1. **(A) The Narrows to Long Creek, 2 miles one way**
2. **(A) The Narrows to Lynnhaven River, 5 miles one way.**
3. **(A) The Narrows to Crystal Lake, 1⅓ miles one way**
4. **(A) The Narrows to Laskin Road, 3 miles one way.**

Section 1. (A) The Narrows to Long Creek, 2 miles one way

The water to the north of The Narrows is Broad Bay and to the south is Linkhorn Bay. The waterfront property aside from the State Park is all privately owned. Please respect the rights of private landholders. Be aware that the channel at The Narrows is heavily used by motor boaters. This is a very populated area. Nevertheless, there is a lot of beautiful shoreline to view by boat. Staying closer to shore and out of boating channels is recommended for safety. It can be very dangerous to be in the way of large yachts that cannot stop quickly or in a channel with fast moving personal watercraft. There are no designated swimming beaches in this area.

This shoreline paddle is breathtaking. Start by paddling north from The Narrows and stick to the north shore. There are high relic dunes presenting pure white beaches right down to the water, backed by majestic tall pines and live oaks. There is a perfect picnic spot here on the north side of the waterway. You can't miss it. Look for the white sand "cliff."

Relic dunes along Broad Bay, First Landing State Park

vs

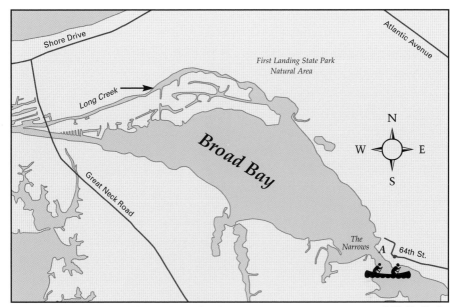

Map 27: The Narrows, Broad Bay and Long Creek   *© Vickie Shufer*

Travel a bit down Long Creek but be aware that the closer you get to the Lynnhaven, the greater the tidal currents. The two channels of Long Creek connect Broad Bay to Lynnhaven Bay. There is a lot of boat traffic near the Lynnhaven and near the marinas. Although there are restaurants and marinas along Long Creek, including a city marina, few have easy access for canoes or kayaks. The best paddling is east of the Long Creek Bridge so just turn around when it comes into view. Paddle around Broad Bay and watch for dolphins during late summer. Local residents report seeing them just off their docks.

Sandy beach at The Narrows   *vs*

Enjoy watching various marsh and shorebirds including osprey, cormorants, brown pelicans, laughing gulls and even an occasional scoter, a sea duck with entirely black plumage and a bright orange-yellow knob on its bill. Absent for many years, bald eagles have again been documented in the area. A pair took up official residence in a secluded section of First Landing State Park to nest and raise their young.

Notice the high banks on the south shore of this area, which are relic dunes and a geologic reminder of this historic area.

Bald Eagles at nest   *Photo by Dennis Bowden*

American Indians spent summers here for many hundreds of years before colonization by the English. Called the Great Neck by the settlers, this high ridge of land has been the site of a great many archaeological digs.

Returning to Broad Bay and heading east then south, the take-out is where you put in, at The Narrows.

Great egret and mallards amongst the cordgrass community   *vs*

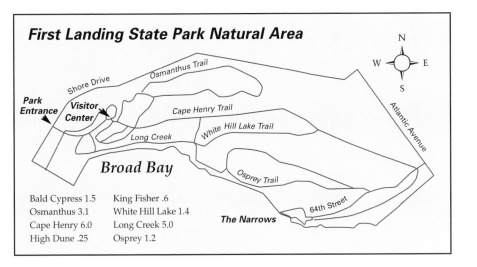

First Landing State Park Natural Area

N
W — E
S

Osmanthus Trail
Shore Drive
Park Entrance
Visitor Center
Cape Henry Trail
White Hill Lake Trail
Long Creek
Broad Bay
Osprey Trail
Atlantic Avenue
64th Street
The Narrows

Bald Cypress 1.5   King Fisher .6
Osmanthus 3.1   White Hill Lake 1.4
Cape Henry 6.0   Long Creek 5.0
High Dune .25   Osprey 1.2

First Landing State Park

First Landing State Park is one of the six original state parks that was built by the Civilian Conservation Corps in the 1930s and was dedicated in 1936 as Seashore State Park. Its name was changed to First Landing State Park in 1997 to reflect its heritage of being near the site where the settlers first landed in 1607. Due to its biodiversity it was designated as a National Natural Landmark in 1967. The Natural Area is located on the south side of Shore Drive while the campground is located on the north side on the Chesapeake Bay. In addition to camping, the park also has cabins available for rent on the south side of Shore Drive near the park entrance.

Today, First Landing consists of 2,888 acres and is the most visited park in the state. It has more than 19 miles of hiking/biking trails that leads visitors through maritime forests, upland forests, swamps, and marshes. The park is open year-round from sunrise to sunset. There is a parking fee to visit the park. For more information call 757-412-2300 or visit www.dcr.virginia.gov.

Swamp Scene   Photo by Dennis Bowden

Section 2. (A) The Narrows to Lynnhaven River, 5 miles one way.

For experienced paddlers and those accustomed to sharing a waterway with motorboat traffic, the trip through Long Creek adds another three miles and includes a trip across Lynnhaven Inlet. The currents through this section are treacherous and we urge caution. The area is highly populated and the homes are beautiful.

The creek is actually two creeks, but before artificially straightened and opened several decades ago, the original Long Creek was a narrow fast-current saltwater feeder to Broad Bay. The opening of the second creek diffused the current somewhat, but both channels now flow quickly with the ebb and

"New" Long Creek, 1930s **Collection of Anne Henry**

flow of the tides. Paddling close to the bulkheaded shoreline will probably be safer than paddling in the center of the canal.

The map below shows the original course of Long Creek. Notice the prominent "Duck Head" that is Cape Henry. Also interesting on this map is what appears to be a road leading to The Narrows from the west and continuing to the east. On a map from the 1866, there is a bridge joining the two land masses here. A 1939 soil map no longer shows a roadway leading to The Narrows or a bridge.

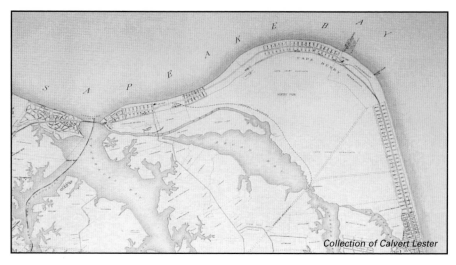

Collection of Calvert Lester

156

Right before entering Lynnhaven Bay there are some waterfront restaurants on the north side, but access to them is really designed for motor boats, not canoes and kayaks. If one's balance is good, take out at one of these restaurants' docks and enjoy some of Virginia Beach's finest seafood. We have often parked a car at one of the restaurants, run a shuttle to First Landing State Park and paddled to brunch and cartopped our kayaks home.

If paddling across Lynnhaven Inlet, be very careful because of current and motorized traffic. The take-out point is Crab Creek to the City's Lynnhaven Boat and Beach Facility operated by the Virginia Beach Department of Parks and Recreation. Use the sandy beach instead of the ramp. This public launch site was completed in the late fall of 2001 and dedicated on May 10, 2002.

Public Facility at Crab Creek   *vs*

Cautionary Notes

Although there are no long fetches, the water in these bays can be quite rough during strong easterly or northerly winds. The mean lunar tides are from 1 to 2 feet, but coastal flooding is common with these high winds. Always check the weather before planning a trip or venturing out.

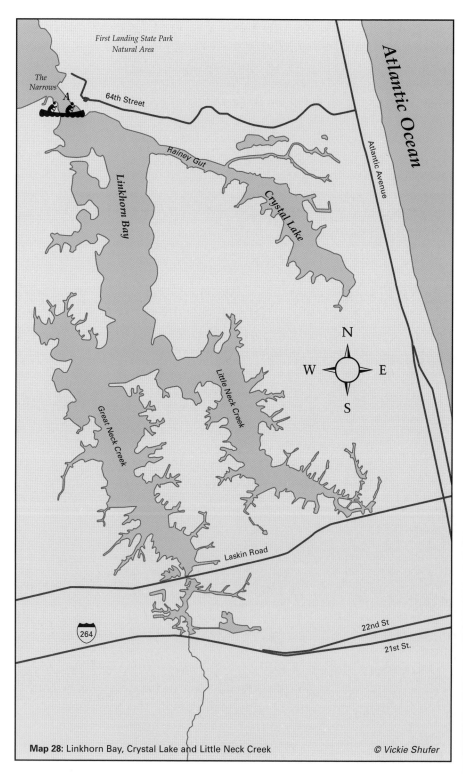

Map 28: Linkhorn Bay, Crystal Lake and Little Neck Creek

© Vickie Shufer

Section 3. (A) The Narrows to Crystal Lake, 1½ miles

Paddle south from "The Narrows" at the end of 64th Street along the closest shoreline through Rainey Gut and into Crystal Lake. This is a short, scenic trip along the park boundary into a beautiful neighborhood of waterfront homes. The take-out for this section is back at the access site, at "The Narrows."

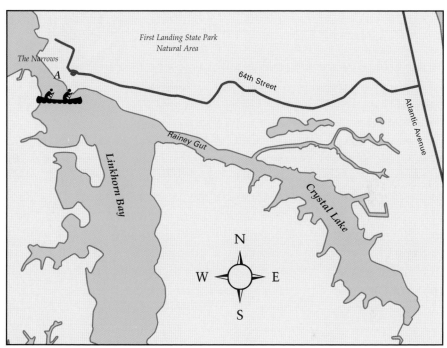

Map 29: The Narrows to Crystal Lake   © Vickie Shufer

Entrance to Rainey Gut/Anna Kephart paddling in front of pine affected by erosion   vs & lg

Salt Plants
Saltwort (*Salicornia* spp.)

Along the edges of the salt marshes growing
amongst the cordgrasses is a plant that looks
different from all the others. It is a succulent
plant with jointed stems and no leaves.
Toward the end of the summer and into the fall,
some plants develop a reddish look. If you break
off one of the jointed stems and bite into it, you will
taste a familiar salty taste, giving it the common
name saltwort. Other names include glasswort, pickle-
weed and marsh samphire.

Saltwort is one of the first plants to colonize on bare tidal flats. A
member of the goosefoot family, it is characterized by succulent stems with
leaves that are reduced to blunt scales, an adaptation to conserve water and
protect themselves from dehydration in the harsh environment where they
grow. Lashed by salt winds and in some cases, immersed by incoming tides,
they remain in place by spreading their roots underground to form a mat that
prevents them from being uprooted by tidal waters. Minute green flowers are
inconspicuous and borne in the hollows of the upper joints, followed by small
seeds.

An interesting use of Salicornia may be responsible for one of its common
names, "Glasswort." Glassmakers would gather the plants, dry them and
then burn them in a large heap. The ashes were combined with sand to make
a rough glass or leached with limewater to make a solution of caustic soda.
Once the moisture had evaporated, crystals of fairly pure sodium hydroxide
remained. This would make a clearer glass or could be used with animal fats
to make soap (Mabey, 1977).

Waterfowl that come here during the winter months, including Canada
and snow geese, feed on the succulent stems. Gadwall, pintail and scaup eat
the seed-bearing tips (Martin, Zim, Nelson, 1951).

Orach   *vs*

Orach

Saltwort is not the only plant from
which salt can be obtained. Another
member of the goosefoot family,
orache also grows in salt marshes
and has a salty taste as well. The
young leaves and tips can be used
like spinach.

160

Notable Dwellings along Crystal Lake

Along this Crystal Lake paddling tour, the paddler can't help but recognize the three story "Greystone Manor House." Less noticed is a Frank Lloyd Wright designed house.

Greystone Manor

The three-story "Greystone Manor" house on the shore of Crystal Lake can be easily seen from the road or from the water. Completed in 1908, this private home was once part of a 130-acre tract that included 800 feet on the oceanfront. The "manor" house is built of stone that the original

lg

owner, Dr. John Masury, imported from Scotland. A cedar boardwalk once bridged the house to the ocean (Mansfield, 1989). The original half-mile boardwalk from the house to a small beachfront cottage was remarkable for its time in that it was not only covered but it was lighted (Goldfarb, 1995). Other amenities included in this "mansion in the wilderness" were a pipe organ located in the attic from which music was piped into every room and an elevator, truly an exotic device for an isolated location. The ballroom could accommodate 200 people and this feature made the house perfect for its next proprietors.

During the 1930s a group of businessmen from North Carolina leased the property and the 25-room dwelling became the "Crystal Club," a nightclub/casino. During this era a spur line of the railroad from Norfolk came directly to the property. By 1942, the house had been bought by William Wilder and Greystone Manor became the old house's new name. Locals have also referred it to as "Greystone Castle." The current owners have occupied the house since the 1981. In 1997, this grand dwelling was added to the National Register of Historic Places. Please respect the property holders' privacy.

Hemicycle Home

Also interior to Crystal Lake is a Frank Lloyd Wright house designed in 1952 and completed in 1959. It was built for Andrew and Maude Cooke as a vacation home in Virginia Beach. Its design is a hemicycle with a curving deck area overlooking a pool. Hidden mostly by vegetation, the house is testament to the current owners' concern for privacy. Please be respectful and do not intrude on private property.

Stratton's Creek

This area called Crystal Lake may have once been part of an inlet into the Atlantic Ocean. Looking at a map of the area it is easy to imagine and anyone who has lived in the vicinity of 56th Street can tell of flooding along Atlantic Avenue many times during heavy rains. On several old maps, including the 1651 Farrer map, is a creek near today's First Landing State Park called Stratten's Creek. On the 1651 map it shows a distinct opening to the ocean, but it may have not been an actual inlet since there are no mentions of an outlet to the ocean in the early grants (that these authors can find). It was in 1638 that John Stratton was granted land from the Lynnhaven to Linkhorn Bay, or "Lincolne" Bay, as it is spelled on a 1695 map. On this same map, Long Creek was "sometimes called Stratton's'," and Broad Bay was "Battses Bay," spelled "Batfses" on a 1711 land grant. The latter was allegedly named for a mariner named Batts (Kellam & Kellam, 1958). One can also locate "Chrystal" Lake on the 1695 map (*The Beach*, 1996). The Kellums write this tantalizing theory which follows in their 1959 book, *Old Houses in Princess Anne Virginia*.

Collection of Lillie Gilbert

In discussing the location of Stratton's Creek as an inlet from the ocean, residents of Princess Anne tell us that there are several characteristics of the sand at this point which differentiate it from the rest of the coast in the immediate vicinity. Hereabouts on the sea side after digging to a certain depth, a stratum of clay is reached. This is not true at the point where we believe this creek found an outlet into the ocean. Here one may continue to dig, but only sand is turned up. Older heads and wiser heads than ours tell us that this is indicative of an opening, which long ago filled by shifting sands. Also we are told that during an unusually severe storm some years ago, the ocean came near breaking through at this point.

While we may never know the whole story behind Stratton's Creek, what we do know is that weather and tidal forces continue to work on our coastlines, opening and closing inlets. For now, the true story of Stratton's Creek remains a mystery.

Section 4. (A) The Narrows to Laskin Road, 3 miles one way

Paddling south from The Narrows into Linkhorn Bay is also a popular playground for motor boats, so be aware. There is no public access at Laskin Road so plan to take out back at The Narrows or plan ahead with a shuttle to a waterfront restaurant along Laskin Road. Scout this ahead of time for permission to park and use as a take-out. This is still an interesting round trip with many large beautiful waterfront homes.

Linkhorn Bay divides into Little Neck Creek to the east and Great Neck Creek to the west. At the tip of the Bird Neck between the two creeks and extending most of its length is the waterfront Cavalier Golf Club and Yacht Club. Along Little Neck Creek to the east is the Princess Anne Country Club. Little Neck Creek effectively ends at Laskin Road. If time allows, plan a trip with a shuttle car located at one of the waterfront restaurants along Laskin Road and combine a paddling day with dinner. If not running a shuttle, paddle to The Narrows as the take-out point as there is no designated public access on Linkhorn Bay proper or Laskin Road.

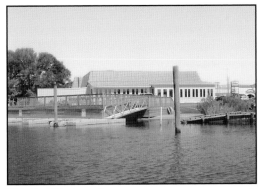

Waterfront Restaurant   *lg*

If paddling Great Neck Creek, go under Laskin Road and after a little over a quarter mile, there is an informal take-out site at the western terminus of Old Virginia Beach Boulevard. This will be on your right as you are heading south on Great Neck Creek. It will be seen just before the power lines and before I-264 crosses the waterway. Parking is limited to one or two cars. If it is not feasible to take-out here, head back to The Narrows.

Lynnhaven Oysters

One can almost imagine the land and waterways as they may have looked to the American Indians who called this area home or those early mariners who saw this land in the sixteenth and seventeenth centuries. By their shell middens all over the Chesapeake Bay we know the American Indians ate many large oysters. By 1816, Chesapeake oysters were being shipped to New York. Later still, the Lynnhaven oyster made quite a name for itself and was featured on menus all along the coast. Diamond Jim Brady in 1898 was said to start a meal with a gallon of orange juice and six dozen Lynnhaven oysters (Kurlansky, 2006). Closed to shell fishing in the 1970s, there may soon be Lynnhaven oysters on menus. Recently good news for the Lynnhaven oyster was announced, "As of November, 2007, 1462 acres of Broad Bay were OPENED to shellfish consumption due to reduced bacterial concentrations" (Lynnhaven River NOW, 2007).

Lynnhaven River NOW

Lynnhaven River NOW began in 2003 with a group of local residents who have one goal – to restore the health of the Lynnhaven River. Partnering with the City of Virginia Beach, the Chesapeake Bay Foundation and the U.S. Army Corps of Engineers, they have undertaken significant projects which include buffer restoration, restoring oyster reefs and salt marsh habitats and promoting public awareness of the river's problems. For information on programs and how you can help support the Lynnhaven River NOW's efforts to clean up the river, call 757-962-5398 or visit lynnhavenrivernow.org.

Interesting Virginia Beach Facts

Virginia Beach is comprised of 248 square miles of land and 59 square miles of water. The average elevation is 12 feet above sea level.

"Virginia Beach Economic Development," *Community Profile*, 2007.

Western Branch of the Lynnhaven River

Just to the west of the Lynnhaven Inlet and Crab Creek, past Pleasure House Creek, the Western Branch is the waterway immediately to the southwest, beginning at Hill Point. It is approximately 6.5 miles in length covering about 1,000 acres extending into Mt. Trashmore, a popular city park.

The shoreline is largely developed, with some fringe marsh and artificially stabilized shore. River depths vary between 2 to 10 feet at low water with dredged canals at between 6 and 12 feet at mean low water. Comprised mostly of private property, there are a few sand beaches, but no public swimming areas.

Access to the Western Branch of the Lynnhaven River is from the Lynnhaven Boat and Beach Facility.

Access Point
A. Lynnhaven Inlet at Crab Creek (see page 142)
Directions: From U.S. Route 60/Shore Drive, the Lynnhaven Boat and Beach Facility is located at the southwest side of the Lesner Bridge on U.S. Route 60/Shore Drive and is accessible to motorized and non-motorized boat traffic. The kayak launch area is a small sandy beach just to the right as one enters the parking lot. There is a small fee to park and many amenities at this access site. For additional information, contact the Virginia Beach Department of Parks and Recreation at 757-385-4461.

Paddling Sections

THE WESTERN BRANCH OF THE LYNNHAVEN RIVER
1. (A) Crab Creek to Pleasure House Creek, less than 1 mile, one way
2. (A) Crab Creek to Thalia Creek 3¾ miles one way

Section 1. (A) Crab Creek to Pleasure House Creek, less than 1 mile, one way

Paddle south on Crab Creek to its end. Note that the Lesner Bridge is the opposite direction from this paddling route. Avoid paddling under the bridge as the strong currents are extremely dangerous for kayaks, canoes, and even motorized craft. Several lives have been lost here.

To continue on the paddling route to Pleasure House Creek, turn right (west) at the first opportunity after exiting Crab Creek. The entrance is a water path in a salt marsh. It is in this area that one of the authors once saw several dozen baby sea turtles swimming toward Lynnhaven Bay.

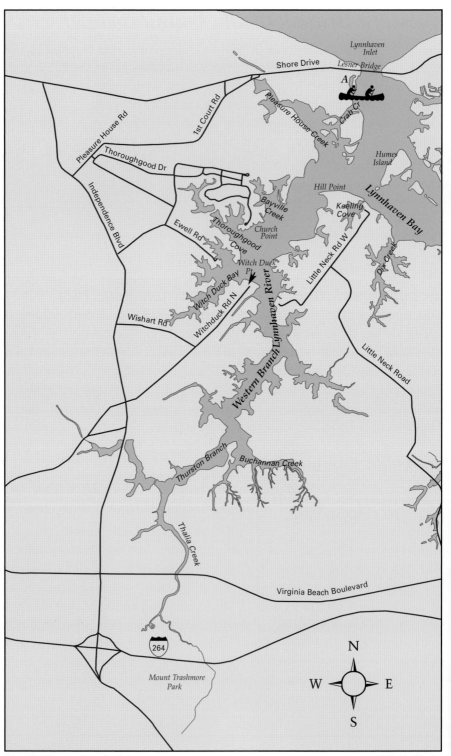

Map 30: Western Branch of the
Lynnhaven River

© Vickie Shufer

Pleasure House Creek, Pleasure House Road and the former Pleasure House Beach are named for a tavern from the 1770s, which was located near the beach until sometime in the 1800s. Too shallow for most power boats, these quiet salt marshes allow for birding from your kayak or canoe. Particularly on a windy day, one can find refuge in the waterways near the Bayville Golf Club built on property that used to be Bayville Dairy Farms. From the water the golf course is barely visible from a canoe or kayak and it is enjoyable to explore the many small waterways that wind through the cordgrass. This is part of the same land originally granted to Adam Thoroughgood in the 1630s.

Although the fishing is good, the area is off-limits for shellfish. The days of the famous Lynnhaven Oyster may be past, but through efforts of Lynnhaven River NOW, the City of Virginia Beach, Virginia Institute of Marine Science, Army Corps of Engineers, Chesapeake Bay Foundation and other volunteer and scholarly groups, every possible effort is being made to restore the Lynnhaven and its tributaries to a purity level that will allow shellfish harvesting once again. If you happen to paddle near some of the new artificial oyster reefs, please do not disturb them.

Out of Crab Creek, if turning to the left (east) and paddling around the southern end of the sand storage area, the paddler is in the strong currents of Lynnhaven Inlet. As tempting as it may be to paddle under the Lesner Bridge and enter the Chesapeake Bay from here, we cannot recommend paddling

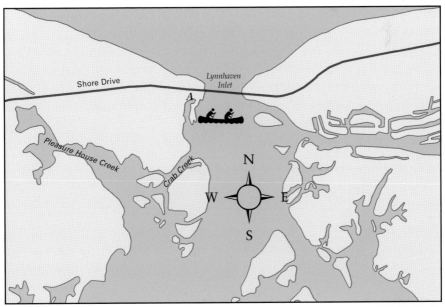

Map 31: Pleasure House Creek   © Vickie Shufer

Lesner Bridge   lg

under this bridge. The currents under the Lesner Bridge are treacherous and many swimmers have lost their lives here. We feel compelled to warn people of the danger. For safety, put in on the bay side if the intent is to paddle in the mouth of the Chesapeake Bay. Try the beach on the northwest side of the Lesner Bridge. Walk your boat along the shoreline or carry or wheel the boat to the northern side of the bridge and paddle west, not east. East will put the paddler back in the swift and dangerous current.

An alternate access point is farther east on Shore Drive at the Lynnhaven Fishing Pier. There is a public access sidewalk to the beach on Starfish Road. This access is a paddler's dream…a short carry, very easy. There is on-street parking at the intersection of Starfish Road and Ocean Shore Avenue where the Lynnhaven Fishing Pier is located, just off Shore Drive (U.S. Route 60). The access is the public access sidewalk and short wooden walkway just to the west of the pier and the Lynnhaven Fish House Restaurant. This beach is fairly narrow but quickly widens east of the pier. We would encourage the paddler to either walk the kayak under the pier to put in or to paddle around the pier to avoid fishing lines. Paddling west from the Lynnhaven Fishing Pier to the Lesner Bridge is under a mile.

One can also launch a kayak from the beach at First Landing State Park on the campground side. Turn north from Shore Drive into the campground and park in the large parking lot west of the contact station. There is a boardwalk trail at the northwest end of the parking lot that will lead one to the public beach. It is almost 2 miles from this beach to the Lynnhaven Fishing Pier. There is a parking fee to use this beach (see page 109 for details).

Lesner Bridge

The original Lesner Bridge was a drawbridge built in 1928 and named for State Senator John A. Lesner of Norfolk. It was replaced in 1958 by a stationary bridge. The second parallel bridge was built many years later and there are future plans for widening the bridges and also to increase the height to accommodate larger vessels. Pedestrian and cyclist lanes are also in the plans.

Section 2. (A) Crab Creek to Thalia Creek, 3¾ miles one way

From Crab Creek, crossing Pleasure House Creek, the paddler will pass Trading Point (now called Hill Point) to the southeast. Many American Indian artifacts have been found here. The small cove here to the southeast is Keeling Cove, named for an early settler.

The next inlet paddling south on the Western Branch is Bayville Creek followed by Church Point, 1⅓ miles from Crab Creek. It is named for the first colonial church built in 1639 by Adam Thoroughgood. The church, abandoned in 1651, was in bad need of repair and the shoreline was eroding. In 1997, underwater archaeologists using sonar located areas where the church grave stones might still be buried in the sand and mud.

The next cove is Thoroughgood Cove, ⁴⁄₁₀ miles south of Church Point. It is named for Captain Adam Thoroughgood, who received a land grant here for 5,350 acres on June 24, 1635 (Nugent, 1992). The English cottage home which is named for the captain was built circa 1703-1719 by one of his descendants and is open to the public. Call 757-460-7588 for tour information. This oldest brick home in Virginia Beach is located at 1636 Parish Road.

Paddling south about ³⁄₁₀ miles, the next series of coves comprise Witch Duck Bay, named for the 1706 trial by water of Grace Sherwood (see p. 80). Back to the Lynnhaven, the paddler, still traveling south, is now only 2 miles from Crab Creek, but the distance may be a lot more if the paddler has gone exploring in the smaller coves. A map and compass or GPS might be useful since it is easy to get disoriented.

Continuing in the Lynnhaven south past Witch Duck Bay, before the river splits into two smaller branches, Ferry Point houses the circa 1830 Ferry Plantation House. It is barely visible from the water and there is no public take-out here, but by calling ahead arrangements might be made for access by kayak and a tour of this antebellum home. Call for details, 757-473-5626.

Another historic house no longer reachable by water is the Lynnhaven House, ca. 1725. This small brick house is considered one of the best preserved colonial dwellings in the U.S. Cared for by the City of Virginia Beach, it is open to visitors at 4405 Wishart Road. Call 757-460-1688 for more information.

The two small tributaries of the Western Branch of the Lynnhaven River marked by Ferry Point are Thurston Branch to the west and Buchannan Creek to the east. Most paddlers call it quits here and retrace the route back to Crab Creek, but if time, please consider exploring these headwaters.

Buchannan Creek, gets pretty shallow over its less than 2 mile length. It is also a populated area, but still pretty with wading birds enjoying the fishing there.

Thurston Branch ends at Thalia Creek. An additional 2 miles along Thalia

Creek will take the paddler to Lake Windsor at Mount Trashmore. This area is heavily populated, but still nice paddling. A fine waterfront restaurant along this route is **Steinhilber's Thalia Acres Inn** located at 653 Thalia Road (by land). Locals rave about the fried

Steinhilber's   *vs*

shrimp as being the finest anywhere. Call first, 757-340-1156, and if you decide to arrive by boat, ask about taking out on the property. There is plenty of parking if you plan a shuttle. Inquire about proper attire if staying for dinner and remember to bring a change of clothes.

It is possible to paddle from Steinhilber's (with permission only) to Mount Trashmore but one should pick a time when the tides are high. Traveling along Thalia Creek, the boater will pass Princess Anne High School on the west side of the creek and Thalia Elementary School on the east. Before the creek passes under Virginia Beach Boulevard and not too far from the water is the former location of Camp Ashby, a German POW camp during WWII (Mansfield, 1989).

German POW Camp

Not far from Thalia Creek the former tuberculosis hospital, Tidewater Victory Memorial Hospital, was completed in the winter of 1937. In 1941 when Camp Thalia was built on grounds surrounding the hospital, the Army leased the hospital from the state of Virginia. With the involvement of the United States in World War II, the camp was renamed Camp Ashby. The large former hospital building became the administrative center for the camp. During its operation from 1944-1946 Camp Ashby housed a total of 6,000 German prisoners of war with a peak capacity of 1,788 one year.

Because so much of the work force of Tidewater was absent during the war, the prisoners served the community as a necessary labor force. Only those prisoners who expressed anti-Nazi sentiments were allowed off the grounds to work. They worked on produce and dairy farms, dug ditches and worked as day laborers at the Fort Story Army Base. The workers were given compensation for their work and could spend their stipend for movies shown at the camp or articles from the camp store. After the war ended, in 1950 the Willis Furniture Company purchased the original hospital building (Mansfield, 1989). It is now part of the Willis Furniture complex on Virginia Beach Boulevard.

Lorraine Eaton and Lillie Gilbert on Thalia Creek *VS*

A side trip to the east will place the boater into Thalia's headwaters, a small winding creek with a lot of twists and turns that are fun to navigate with great views of Town Center's skyscrapers. A resident of the area in the 1950s remembers as a child fishing for salt water fish in Thalia's then clear waters and reported seeing muskrats and otter that lived in this stream (Jenkins, 2007). Saltmeadow hay, saltmarsh cordgrass, black needlerush, marsh fleabane and rose mallows are just some of the marsh plants that can be seen on this part of the trip. Overhead osprey, kingfishers, herons and egrets can sometimes be observed.

As you approach the Interstate bridges, you will notice a difference in the current. If the tide is coming in, you will be carried along, almost like paddling white water. Otherwise, you will have to work against the current, which can be pretty strong. After going under the Interstate bridges, you will come to Mount Trashmore. There is no designated take-out point. If you plan to take out here, use caution as the banks can be slippery.

Culverts under I-264 *VS*

Saltmarsh Wildflowers

Hidden among the cordgrasses and out of the reach of the tides are a number of colorful wildflowers that make their appearance in mid-summer and continue into the autumn. These native wildflowers are specially adapted to this environoment and are tolerant of the salt spray and an occasional inundation of the salty water. The flowers are a source of nectar for bees and other pollinating insects.

Seashore Mallow   *lg*

New York Aster   *vs*

Sea Oxeye   *vs*

Saltmarsh Fleabane   *vs*

The Canal That Never Was

In 1840, the Princess Anne and Kempsville Canal Company was incorporated to connect the headwaters of the Elizabeth River's Eastern Branch, at Kempsville, to those of the Lynnhaven River. The State took part of the company's stock and civil engineer Claudius Crozet (who later gained fame as the creator of the 1858 Blue Ridge parkway railroad tunnel at Rockfish Gap) carried out the surveys necessary to make the cut. The charter for this canal was amended several times and by 1861 the company now reorganized as the Kempsville Canal Company began work. Digging of the 4 mile canal was started but the Civil War put a halt to the project, which was never completed (Brown, 1981). The project faded into obscurity and the few excavated remnants can be seen only in Kempsville by paddling from the Carolanne Farm Park launch site on Challedon Drive. For information on this canoe/kayak launch site contact Virginia Beach Park Operations at 757-385-4461. One can only wonder might have become of the areas that were to be connected with a commercial waterway had this project been competed.

Mount Trashmore Park

Mount Trashmore, dedicated in 1972, was the first landfill in the nation constructed to become a public park. It was constructed during five years' worth of layering solid waste and clean soil. At over 800 feet long and 60 feet tall, Mt. Trashmore is the currently the highest point of land in the city. A new landfill "mountain," which when completed will become part of City View Park in the Kempsville area of Virginia Beach, is being constructed in a similar manner. It will be taller than Mt. Trashmore upon its completion in a few years. Both parks are managed by the Virginia Beach Department of Parks and Recreation.

The two lakes at Mount Trashmore, Windsor and Trashmore, are considered as retention ponds for drainage for the closest neighborhoods, streets and the park. Thalia Creek feeds Lake Windsor so the water is slightly brackish. Lake Trashmore is a freshwater lake. These two lakes are currently closed to paddlers. The 165 acre park is the city's most popular and the site of a variety of recreational activities from private picnics to large festivals. The park contains picnic shelters, skate park, playgrounds, basketball courts, volleyball areas, Kids' Cove, walking paths, a xeriscape garden, vending machines, restrooms and is handicapped accessible. Call 757-385-4461 for more information.

Appendix A - City Code for Launching Boats in Virginia Beach

Sec. 6-114. Restrictions on launching, landing, parking or stationing recreational vessels in certain areas.

(a) It shall be unlawful for any person to launch or land a sailboat, motorboat, motorized personal watercraft, canoe, rowboat, flatboat, kayak, umiak, scull or any other similar recreational vessel on the beach area north of Rudee Inlet to the center line of 42nd Street prolongated eastward, during the resort season between the hours of 10:00 a.m. and 4:00 p.m. weekdays and 10:00 a.m. and 6:00 p.m. weekends and holidays. The provisions of this subsection shall not be applicable to any person who is awarded a contract, based upon competitive procurement principles, to conduct an operation for the rental of designated recreational vessel(s) or to any person who rents a vessel from an authorized rental operator provided the vessel(s) so rented is launched or landed within the area designated in such contract.

(b) It shall be unlawful for any person to park or station a sailboat, motorboat, motorized personal watercraft, canoe, rowboat, flatboat, kayak, umiak, scull or other similar recreational vessel on the beach area north of Rudee Inlet to the center line of 42nd Street prolongated eastward, with the following exceptions:

   (1) In an emergency;

   (2) With an approved race or regatta permit;

   (3) In the process of launching or landing a vessel specified above in the areas and during the time periods permitted in subsection (a) of this section; or

   (4) Pursuant to a contract in accordance with the provisions of subsection (a) of this section.

(c) It shall be unlawful for any person to launch, land, park or station a motorboat or motorized personal watercraft on the beach between the area north of the center line of 42nd Street prolongated eastward and the southern boundary line of Fort Story, except in an emergency or with an approved race or regatta permit.

(d) It shall be unlawful for any person to launch or land any motorboat, motorized personal water craft or any other motorized recreational vessel on the beaches extending south of Fleet Combat Training Center Dam Neck to the southern boundary of Little Island Park, or on the beaches south of Rudee Inlet to the northern boundary of Camp Pendleton Military Reservation, during the season from 6:00 p.m. on the Friday before Memorial Day Weekend through 6:00 p.m. on the Monday following Labor Day Weekend, between the hours of 10:00 a.m. and 4:00 p.m. weekdays and 10:00 a.m. and 6:00 p.m. weekdays and 10:00 a.m. and 6:00 p.m. weekends and holidays, except as hereafter provided:

   (1) Watercraft may be launched or landed in an emergency or for law enforcement purposes.

(2) Commercial fishing boats operating from the beaches by permission of the Virginia Division of Parks and Recreation shall be exempt from the restrictions of this article.

(e) It shall be unlawful for any person to launch, land, park or station a sailboat, motorboat, motorized personal watercraft, canoe, rowboat, flatboat, kayak, umiak, scull or any other similar recreational vessel on the beach area between the western end of the Lesner Bridge continuing southwest along the shoreline of the Lynnhaven Turning Basin and then west to the Lynnhaven Boat Ramp at Crab Creek with the following exceptions:

(1) In an emergency; or

(2) With an approved race or regatta permit.

(f) In addition to the other provisions of this section, sailboats parked on the beach shall be subject to the following restrictions:

(1) It shall be unlawful to park or station a sailboat on any sand dune or in front of any access point or street end.

(2) It shall be unlawful to drive any type of anchor into the beach to secure a sailboat, unless approved by the director of the department of public works as to type, size and location.

(3) It shall be unlawful to secure a sailboat to fixtures or structures on the beach.

(g) Any police officer of the City of Virginia Beach is hereby authorized to remove and impound or have removed and impounded any vessel which appears to be in violation of this section or which is lost, stolen, abandoned or unclaimed. In addition to the fine imposed for a violation of this section, such vessel shall be removed and impounded at the owner's expense until lawfully claimed or disposed of.

(h) Any person who shall violate any of the provisions of this section shall be guilty of a Class 4 misdemeanor.

(Code 1965, § 6-13; Ord. No. 1033, 4-21-80; Ord. No. 1037, 5-12-80; Ord. No. 1150, 3-9-81; Ord. No. 1909, 8-21-89; Ord. No. 2055, 4-23-91; Ord. No. 2087, 7-9-91; Ord. No. 2103, 9-3-91; Ord. No. 2126, 4-28-92; Ord. No. 2227, 5-23-93; Ord. No. 2736, 2-25-03; Ord. No. 2868, 4-26-05; Ord. No. 2901, 11-22-05)

Sec. 6-120. Boating, skiing, etc., prohibited in marked swimming areas.

(a) Except in the case of an emergency, it shall be unlawful for any person to operate a motorboat, water skis, motorized water transportation or any self-propelled vehicle, surfboard or other similar device within the area of water designated and marked as provided in Section 6-16.

(b) A violation of this section shall be punished by a fine of not more than fifty dollars ($50.00).

(Code 1965, § 6-16; Ord. No. 1370, 4-25-83)

State law references: Similar provisions, Code of Virginia, §§ 62.1-180, 62.1-185.

Appendix B - References

Barrow, Mary Reed. June 2, 1985. "German POWs Served Time on County's Farms." *The Beacon*, Norfolk, VA: Landmark Communications.

——. May 26, 2002. "Eagle Pair Set Up Housekeeping in First Landing State Park." *The Beacon*, Norfolk, VA: Landmark Communications.

Bisher, Catherine W. and Southern, Michael T. 1996. *A Guide to Architecture of Eastern North Carolina*. Chapel Hill, NC: The University North Carolina Press.

Boyd, William K. 1929. *Introduction to the First Edition, History of the Dividing Line*. North Carolina Historical Commission. Republished 1969 by Dover Publications, Inc., New York, NY, with a new Introduction by Percy G. Adams.

Brown, Alexander Crosby. 1981. *Juniper Waterway*. Charlottesville, VA: University of Virginia Press.

Cecelski, David. 2000. *A Historian's Coast*. Winston-Salem, NC: John F. Blair, Publisher.

City of Virginia Beach. 2002. *Beaches and Waterways Commission Report*. Virginia Beach, VA: City of Virginia Beach.

City of Virginia Beach Department of Parks and Recreation. Summer, 1998. "Where Does the Water Go?" *Naturally Speaking*. Virginia Beach, VA: Department of Parks and Recreation

Creecy, John Harvie, editor. 1954. *Virginia Antiquary*. Volume I, Princess Anne County Loose Papers, 1700-1789, Richmond, VA, The Dietz Press, Inc.

Currituck County Tricentennial Committee. 1970. "Twenty Ways to Spell Currituck," Currituck County Tricentennial, 1670 – 1970.

Currituck Wild Horse Fund. 2004. http://www.co.currituck.nc.us/leisure/attractions/wild_horse/Wild%20Horse%20advertisement.pdf.

Davis, Marc. October 26, 1997. "Inlet Faces Unknown Soundings Since 1927." *The Virginian Pilot*. Norfolk, Va: Landmark Communications.

Emmerson, John C. Jr. May 19, 1826. "Steam Navigation in Virginia and Northeastern North Carolina Waters, 1826- 1836." *The Norfolk and Portsmouth Herald*. Portsmouth, Virginia, 1949.

Erichsen-Brown, Charlotte. 1979. *Medicinal and Other Uses of North American Plants*. New York: Dover Publications, Inc.

Evans-Hylton, Patrick. March 10, 2002. "City's Mounted Patrol Moves into Its New Permanent Home." *The Beacon.* Norfolk, VA:Landmark Communications.

Everts, C.H.; Battley Jr., J.P.; and Gibson, P.N. 1983. *Shoreline Movements: Report 1; Cape Henry, Virginia, to Cape Hatteras, North Carolina, 1849-1980.* Technical Report CERC-83-, Report 1, U.S. Army Corps of Engineers.

Fischer, David Hackett and Kelly, James C. 2000. *Bound Away, Virginia and the Westward Movement.* Charlottesville, VA: The University Press of Virginia.

Forrest, William S. 1853. *Historical and Descriptive Sketches of Norfolk and Vicinity.* Philadelphia, PA: Lindsay and Blakiston.

Gilbert, Lillie and Shufer, Vickie. 2004. *Wild River Guide to Dismal Swamp Water Trails.* Virginia Beach, VA: Eco Images.

Gilbert, Lillie and Shufer, Vickie. 2001. *Wild River Guide to the North Landing River and Its Tributaries.* Virginia Beach, VA: Eco Images.

Goldfarb, Greg. April 28, 1995. "Owners of Greystone Mansion seek tax relief." *Beacon.* Norfolk, VA: Landmark Publications, Inc.

Hanbury, Elizabeth Baum. 1985. *Currituck Legacy, The Baum Family of North Carolina.* Chesapeake, VA.

Henderson, Archibald. 1941. *North Carolina, The Old North State and the New,* Volume II. Chicago: The Lewis Publishing Company.

Henry, Anne. October 25, 2007, unpublished document, used by permission.

—— October 28, 2007. Personal communication.

Hugo, Nancy. October, 1987. "Virginia's Wild Rice." *Virginia Wildlife.*

Jenkins, David. October 22, 2007. Personal communication.

Kaufman, Wallace and Pilkey, Orrin. 1979. *The Beaches Are Moving.* Garden City, NY: Anchor Press/Doubleday.

Kellam, Sadie Scott and Kellam, V. Hope. 1958. *Old Houses in Princess Anne Virginia.* Portsmouth, VA: Printcraft Press, Inc.

Kight, John R. 1990. *The Cape Henry Threshold.* Virginia Beach, VA.

Kurlansky, Mark. 2006. *The Big Oyster, History on the Half Shell.* New York: Ballantine Books.

Kyle, Louisa Venable. 1969. *The History of Eastern Shore Chapel and Lynnhaven Parish 1642-1969.* Norfolk, VA: Teagle and Little, Inc.

Kyle, Louisa V. April 15, 1956. *A Country Woman's Scrapbook.* Norfolk, VA: Norfolk Virginian Pilot.

Lukei, Melinda. Unpublished document.

Lukei, Reese. Unpublished document.

—— Unpublished document.

—— May 11, 2007. Personal communication.

Lynnhaven River NOW. Press Release. November, 2007. Virginia Beach, VA: Lynnhaven River NOW.

Malec, Pam. 2001. *Guide to Sea Kayaking in North Carolina*. Guilford, CT: The Globe Pequot Press.

Maling, Anne E. 1992. *Princess Anne Co. VA Land & Probate Records, Abstracted from Deed Books 1-7, 1691-1755*, p. 5. Bowie, MD: Heritage Books.

Mansfield, Stephen S. 1989. *Princess Anne County and Virginia Beach, A Pictorial History*. Norfolk, VA: The Donning Company.

Martin, Alexander C., Zim, Herbert S. and Nelson, Arnold L. 1951. *American Wildlife & Plants - A Guide to Wildlife Food Habits*. New York: Dover Publications, Inc.

McEwen, W.A. and Lewis, A.H. 1953. *Encyclopedia of Nautical Knowledge*. Cambridge, MD: Cornell Maritime Press.

Middleton, Arthur Pierce. 1984. *Tobacco Coast, A Maritime History of Chesapeake Bay in the Colonial Era*. Baltimore, MD: The Johns Hopkins University Press.

Miles, Dr.D.W.H. and Worthington, M.J. December 2006. *Tree Ring Dating of the Adam Keeling House*. Virginia Beach, VA, South Oxfordshire, England: Oxford Dendrochronology Laboratory.

Morris, Travis, 2006. *Duck Hunting on Currituck Sound, Tales from a Native Gunner*. Charleston, SC: The History Press.

Needham, William. 2006. *Hiker's Notebook*. www.mwrop.org/_Needham/h_notebook.html.

NOAA website. 2002. www.noaanews.noaa.gov.

Nugent, Nell Marion. 1992. *Cavaliers and Pioneers, Abstracts of Virginia Land Patents and Grants, Volume I, 1623-1666*. Richmond, VA: Virginia State Library.

Nugent, Nell Marion. 1977. *Cavaliers and Pioneers, Abstracts of Virginia Land Patents and Grants, Volume II, 1666-1695*. Richmond, VA: Virginia State Library.

Parker, Stacy. January 19, 2003. "Hunt Room Atmosphere Is So Delightful." *Virginia Beach Beacon*. Norfolk, VA: Landmark Communications.

Perry, Bill. 1985. *A Sierra Club Naturalist's Guide to The Middle Atlantic Coast: Cape Hatteras to Cape Cod*. San Francisco: Sierra Club Books.

Pouliot, Richard A. and Pouliot, Julie J. 1986. *Shipwrecks on the Virginia Coast and the Men of the Life-Saving Service*. Centreville, MD: Tidewater Publishers.

Powell, William S. 1958. *Ye Countie of Albemarle in Carolina, A Collection of Documents 1664-1675*. Raleigh, NC: NC State Department of Archives and History.

Quinn, David Beers. 1991. *The Roanoke Voyages 1584-1590, Volume I*. Mineola, NY: Dover publications, Inc.

Rountree, Helen C. 1989. *The Powhatan Indians of Virginia*. Norman, OK: University of Oklahoma Press.

Tate, Suzanne. 1987. *Whalehead: Tales of Corolla, N.C.* Nags Head, NC: Nags Head Art.

Tazewell, C.W., Jr., Editor, 1982. *Walke Family Scrapbook*. Virginia Beach, VA:

Tennant, Diane. December 2, 2001. "Swept Away, Shifting Sands Cover What Once Was Seagull, N.C.." *The Virginian Pilot*, Norfolk, VA:Landmark Communications, Inc.

Turner, Florence Kimberly. 1984. *Gateway to the New World: A History of Princess Anne County, Virginia 1607-1824*. Early, SC: Southern Historical Press, Virginia Department of Game & Inland Fisheries. 1989. *Wading Birds of the Virginia Shores*.

Virginia Beach News. August 1, 1947. "Emmanuel Church in 104th Year." Virginia Beach VA.

Virginia Beach Public Library. 1996. *The Beach. Virginia Beach, VA: Department of Public Libraries, City of Virginia Beach*.

Virginia Department of Game and Inland Fisheries. 1989. *Wading Birds of the Virginia Shores*.

Virginian-Pilot. June 21, 2002. "New Methanol-Based Fuel Cell Now Powers Lighthouse." Norfolk, VA: Landmark Communications.

Virtual Jamestown. 2000, http://etext.lib.virginia.edu/etcbin/jamestown-browse?id=J1002

Whichard, Rogers Dey. 1959. *The History of Lower Tidewater Virginia. Volume II*, New York, NY: Lewis Historical Publishing Company, Inc.

Appendix C - Organizations

Adam Thoroughgood House
1636 Parish Road
Virginia Beach, VA 23455
(757) 460-7588

Association for the Preservation of Virginia Antiquities
(804) 648-1889
www.apva.org

Atlantic Wildfowl Heritage Museum and the Back Bay Wildfowl Guild, Inc.
1113 Atlantic Avenue
Virginia Beach, VA 23451
(757) 437-8432
www.awhm.org

Back Bay National Wildlife Refuge
4005 Sandpiper Road
Virginia Beach, VA 23456
(757) 721-2412
www.fws.gov/backbay

Back Bay Restoration Foundation
3022 New Bridge Road
Virginia Beach, VA 23456
bbrf@verizon.net
(757) 721-7666
www.bbrf.org

Chesapeake Bay Program
(800) YOUR-BAY
www.chesapeakebay.net

Chesapeake Bay Center
2500 Shore Drive
Virginia Beach, VA 23451
(757) 412-2316

Corolla Wild Horse Fund, Inc.
PO Box 361, Corolla, NC 27927
(252) 453-8002
www.corollawildhorses.com.

Currituck Beach Light House/ Outer Banks Conservationists
P.O. Box 58
Corolla, NC 27927
(252) 453-4939
www.currituckbeachlight.com

Currituck National Wildlife Refuge
P.O. Box 39
Knotts Island, NC 27950
http://www.fws.gov

False Cape State Park
4001 Sandpiper Road
Virginia Beach, VA 23456
(757) 426-3657
www.dcr.state.va.us/parks

Ferry Plantation House
4136 Cheswick Lane
Virginia Beach, VA 23455
(757) 473-5626

First Landing State Park
2500 Shore Drive
Virginia Beach, VA 23451
www.dcr.state.va.us/parks

Francis Land House
3131 Virginia Beach Blvd
Virginia Beach, VA 23452
(757) 431-4000
www.vbgov.com

Lynnhaven House
4405 Wishart Road
Virginia Beach, Va 23455
(757) 460-1688

Lynnhaven River Now
1608 Pleasure House Road Suite 108
Virginia Beach, VA 23455
(757) 962-5398
http://www.lynnhavenriver2007.org

Mackay Island NWR
P.O. Box 39
Knotts Island, NC 27950-0039
(252) 429-3100
http://mackayisland.fws.gov.

North Carolina Coastal Reserve
135 Duke Marine Lab Road
Beaufort, NC 28516
(252) 728-2170
www.ncnerr.org

Outer Banks Center for Wildlife Education
P.O. Box 502
Corolla, NC 27927
(252) 453-0221
www.ncwildlife.org

Outer Banks Lighthouse Society
PO Box 1005
Morehead City, NC 28557
society@outer-banks.com

The Old Coast Guard Station
24th Street & Boardwalk
Virginia Beach, VA 23451
(757) 422-1587
www.oldcoastguardstation.com

Virginia Aquarium and Marine Science Center
717 General Booth Blvd
Virginia Beach, VA 23451
www.virginiaaquarium.com

Virginia Beach Department of Parks and Recreation
2408 Courthouse Drive, Building 21
Virginia Beach, VA 23456

Virginia Beach Historical Society
2040 Potters Road
Virginia Beach, VA 23454
(757) 491-3490
http://virginiabeachhistory.org

Virginia Department of Game and Inland Fisheries
4010 West Broad St
Richmond, VA 23230-1104
(804) 367-1000
www.dgif.virginia.gov

Virginia Tourism Corporation
901 E. Byrd St.
Richmond, VA 23219
www.virginia.org

Whalehead Preservation Trust
P.O. Box 307
Corolla, NC 27927
(252) 453-9040
www.whaleheadclub.com

Appendix D - Plant List

Latin names for plants listed in text by common name

Arrow Arum	*Peltandra virginica*
Aster, New York	*Aster novi-belgii*
Bald Cypress	*Taxodium distichum*
Bayberry	*Myrica cerifera*
Black Gum, Swamp	*Nyssa biflora*
Black Needlerush	*Juncus roemerianus*
Cattail, Common	*Typha latifolia*
Cherry, Black	*Prunus serotina*
Coontail	*Ceratophyllum demersum*
Cordgrass, Big	*Spartina cynosuroides*
Cordgrass, Saltmarsh	*Spartina alterniflora*
Duckweed	*Lemna spp.*
Fleabane, Saltmarsh	*Pluchea purpurascens*
Grape, Muscadine	*Vitis rotundifolia*
Groundsel Bush	*Baccharis halimifolia*
Lotus, American	*Nelumbo lutea*
Mallow, Rose	*Hibiscus moscheutos*
Mallow, Seashore	*Kosteletzkya virginica*
Maple, Red	*Acer rubrum*
Milkweed, Swamp	*Asclepias incarnata*
Orach	*Atriplex patula*
Phragmites	*Phragmites australis*
Pine, Loblolly	*Pinus taeda*
Pondweed, Sago	*Potamogeton pectinatus*
Redhead Grass	*Potamogeton perfoliatus*
Rice Cutgrass	*Leersia oryzoides*
Rice, Wild	*Zizania aquatica*
Rose, Swamp	*Rosa palustris*
Saltmarsh Loosestrife	*Lythrum lineare*
Saltmeadow Hay	*Spartina patens*
Saltwort	*Salicornia spp.*
Sawgrass	*Cladium jamaicense*
Sea Oxeye	*Borrichia frutescens*
Smartweed	*Polygonum spp.*
Sweetgum	*Liquidambar styraciflua*
Water Parsnip	*Sium suave*
Waterlily	*Nymphaea odorata*
Watermilfoil	*Myriophyllum spp.*
Waxmyrtle	*Myrica cerifera*
Widgeongrass	*Ruppia maritima*
Wild Celery	*Vallisneria americana*
Willow, Black	*Salix nigra*
Yaupon Holly	*Ilex vomitoria*

Index

Y

Other Eco Images Titles
of Related Interest

Bayside History Trail
A View From the Water
by Lillie Gilbert, Belinda Nash, & Deni Norred-Williams

ISBN: ISBN: 9780-938423-09-6

Ghosts, Witches & Weird Tales of Virginia Beach
by Lillie Gilbert, Belinda Nash, & Deni Norred-Williams

ISBN: ISBN: 9780-938423-12-6

A Trek to the Top of Mount Kilimanjaro
by Ann Brand, Ed.D.

ISBN: ISBN: 9780-938423-10-2

Getting to Pine Island
an Outer Banks Odyssey
by Elizabeth Baum Hanbury

ISBN: 9780-938423-15-7

If you would like to receive a free catalog featuring additional
Eco Images books, please contact

Eco Images

P.O. Box 61413
Virginia Beach, VA 23466-1413
757.421.3929
EcoImages@cox.net
www.ecoimages-us.com